Small Corroding Words

Small Corroding Words

The slighting of Great Britain by the EHRC

A Rejoinder to
How Fair is Britain? Equality, Human Rights and Good Relations in 2010: the first triennial review, a report by the Equality and Human Rights Commission

Jon Gower Davies

Foreword by
Justin Shaw

Civitas: Institute for the Study of Civil Society
London

First Published July 2011

55 Tufton Street
London SW1P 3QL

email: books@civitas.org.uk

ISBN 978-1-906837-22-8

Typeset by
Civitas

Printed in Great Britain by
Berforts Group Ltd
Stevenage SG1 2BH

This book is dedicated to Norman Dennis,
the best of men

1929 – 2010

Memories

'The eradication of memories of the Great War'

Kipling meditates on the likelihood of 'a socialist government' abolishing Remembrance Day

THOUGH all the Dead were all forgot
And razed were every tomb,
The Worm—the Worm that dieth not
Compels Us to our doom.
Though all which once was England stands
Subservient to Our will,
The Dead of whom we washed Our hands,
They have observance still.

We laid no finger to Their load.
We multiplied Their woes.
We used Their dearly-opened road
To traffic with Their foes:
And yet to Them men turn their eyes,
To Them are vows renewed
Of Faith, Obedience, Sacrifice,
Honour and Fortitude!

Which things must perish. But Our hour
Comes not by staves or swords
So much as, subtly, through the power
Of small corroding words.
No need to make the plot more plain
By any open thrust;
But—see Their memory is slain
Long ere Their bones are dust!

Wisely, but yearly, filch some wreath—
Lay some proud rite aside—
And daily tarnish with Our breath
The ends for which They died.
Distract, deride, decry, confuse—
(Or—if it serves Us—pray!)
So presently We break the use
And meaning of Their day!

Rudyard Kipling, 1930

Contents

Acknowledgements

Thanks are due to David Green, Robert Whelan and Nick Cowen of Civitas; to two anonymous referees: and to Norman Dennis, John Taylor, Ab Hamed and Denis Maceoin for help, advice and companionship over many months.

Extract from 'Church Going' by Philip Larkin © the Estate of Philip Larkin and reproduced by kind permission of Faber and Faber Ltd, London.

Author

Jon Gower Davies retired from the University of Newcastle in 1997. He lectured, first, in the Social Studies Department, and then in the Department of Religious Studies, of which he was Head. For 20 years he was a Labour Councillor on Newcastle City Council. He is the author and editor of books and articles on a wide range of topics, including *Bonfires on the Ice: the multicultural harrying of Britain* and *In Search of the Moderate Muslim,* published by the Social Affairs Unit; *A New Inquisition: religious persecution in Britain today,* published by Civitas; and on attitudes to death and dying in the ancient religions of the world, published by Routledge. He has a particular interest in war and war memorials as definers of what he calls 'Eurochristianity'.

He was born in North Wales. From there, after the war, he went with his family to Kenya, then a British colony. He lived in Mombasa, went to school in Nairobi, and travelled widely throughout East Africa. After a short spell in the Kenya Regiment, a part of the British Army, he left for England to attend Oxford University. Two years in America, which included attending Brandeis University and participating in the 'Freedom Summer' in Mississippi, ended with his return to England. Since 1965, he has lived in Newcastle upon Tyne with his wife Jean. They have three children, who now have children of their own. He is a communicant member of the Church of England.

Foreword

In the opening chapters of *Small Corroding Words,* Jon Gower Davies examines *How Fair is Britain?*, a 750-page report published in 2010 by the Equality and Human Rights Commission (EHRC). This 'first triennial review' presents a massive body of statistical material relating to British society as a whole, and to particular groups within it, defined in ethnic, religious or (less often) sexual terms, with the aim of comparing the condition of the 'majority' to that of selected 'minorities'. From this evidence, the report's authors hope to establish first, how unequal the *outcomes* of British lives are (measured by such things as educational attainment, unemployment rates, income, savings, criminal convictions, health, life-expectancy and so on); and secondly, how unequal the *processes* are by which the British (or subgroups of us) reach these outcomes. In speaking of 'process', the report is concerned with 'inequalities in treatment through discrimination or disadvantage... including lack of dignity or respect'.

The upshot of this search for the intersection between two kinds of measurable inequality is—perhaps unsurprisingly—a negative answer to the question posed in its title: Britain is not fair at all. Yet, as Davies points out, the report's conclusion is undermined by two elementary conceptual errors. First of all, there is a failure to consider what contribution our personal responsibility, choice, or (to use the report's word) *autonomy,* makes to these complex outcomes and processes. Deferring this question to a later publication, the report acknowledges 'autonomy' as 'a critical element in allowing people to flourish', and it is hard to disagree with this: certainly any interpretation of social statistics as evidence of unfairness must involve (among other things) an assessment of agents' autonomy. Indeed, the report's failure to consider the causal contribution of personal choice, proclivity or preference to the sum of human achievement, effectively decouples the question of 'fairness' posed in its title from the various forms of measurable inequality illustrated in its tables and graphs.

The second defect is still more fundamental, and serves to exacerbate the first. The report, Davies points out, fails to provide any form of comparative material, either historic or geographical, by which the British statistics can be meaningfully assessed in relation to those of other societies. It is as though its authors regard the mere fact of differential group outcomes and processes within a population of 60 million as proof in itself of systemic unfairness—even in the absence of evidence that things turn out more equally (or more fairly) in other large societies. In point of fact, as Davies demonstrates, reliable international comparative data are easy enough to come by; and if the authors of *How Fair is Britain?* had sought them out, they would have been able to demonstrate that the British, including the least advantaged groups in Britain, enjoy substantial advantages across a wide range of measurable outcomes compared to the subjects of all but a handful of other wealthy nations.

It does not follow from this that conditions in Britain cannot or should not be improved in various ways. The point, rather, is that an intelligent engagement with comparative data would seem to be a necessary precondition of effective social analysis and reform. More to the present point, such an approach is demanded by the standards of disinterested, sceptical empiricism which ought to be manifest in any serious work of scholarship, and especially so when its authors depend on public sponsorship, and benefit from a degree of official authority.

All in all, it is difficult to avoid the impression that *How Fair is Britain?* actually sets out to demonstrate that Britain is (by some significant, if unexamined standard) thoroughly unfair—an impression reinforced by its selective use of commentary, and a rhetorical tone which is alternately peremptory and evasive. In short, the authors do not need to investigate their subject matter, because the conclusions have been established *a priori*.

In this respect *How Fair is Britain?* takes its place in an established tradition of multicultural literature, the most influential example probably being the Parekh Report, to which Davies devotes a central part of the book.[1] By combining ideas derived from post-modern cultural 'theory'[2] with a strongly deterministic view of history, Parekh presents the case that British society is (indeed, *must* be) racist and discriminatory today because Britain was the instigator of a racist and discriminatory Empire. As one anonymous contributor to the report explains: 'Britain seems incapable of shaking off its imperialist identity. The Brits do appear to believe that "Britons never, never, never shall be slaves"... [But] it is impossible to colonise three fifths of the world... without enslaving oneself.'

The belief that modern British identity has been largely determined and defined by Britain's imperial past is axiomatic to official multiculturalism. And it follows from it that the British (or at any rate, the English), if they are to be redeemed, must confess and repent of their historic sins, purging first themselves, and then their institutions, of racism. 'It is not a question of curing me,' another witness tells the report's authors, 'but of me acknowledging my racism and taking personal responsibility for operating in a non-racist way personally and encouraging organisations and institutions in which I have an influence to do the same.'

Such public self-denunciations—like those elicited from 'undesirable elements' by the totalitarian regimes of the twentieth century—form part of an official and coercive cultural policy. As Parekh argues: 'If Britain is to flourish as a community of citizens and communities, its political leaders should shape, and not pander to, public opinion on issues relating to race and diversity' (see p. 31).[3] And in this respect, the UK courts' expansive interpretation of the doctrine of human rights over the last two decades, and especially since the Human Rights Act (1999), has been of primary importance. 'Equality' and 'Human Rights' have been bound together in a dynamic alliance: one as the official goal of public policy, the other as the principal means of enforcement.

Yet this impressive structure of public control is built on weak intellectual foundations. In the official multicultural view, politics and culture are products of a historic struggle, not principally between economic classes—as in classical Marxism—but between oppressor and victim groups defined by race, religion and sexuality. These conglomerates, understood as more or less undifferentiated blocs, operate in a deterministic universe, subject (especially the 'oppressors') to a high degree of false consciousness, as they compete in a zero-sum game for public funding and recognition. And just as political life, according to this view, is circumscribed by the logic of group conflict, so individual human beings are deprived of much of their complexity, dignity and freedom of choice: often enough, in the multicultural literature, the relationship between the individual and his or her ethnic, religious and cultural inheritance is seen as essentially fixed and unalterable.

This emphasis on historic conflict between groups, and the grievances which divide them, naturally leads Parekh and his followers away from a consideration of the means by which people of different backgrounds and beliefs can (and often do) share important loyalties and commitments. This is particularly so when these loyalties arise from the historic institutions of the British state and society, which, on Parekh's imperialist reading of British history, are assumed *a priori* to be instruments of oppression: 'Britishness,' the report states bluntly, 'as much as Englishness, has systematic, largely unspoken, racial connotations.'[4]

Parekh's 'racialising' of British history turns the relationship between ethnic identity and national consciousness neatly on its head.[5] By claiming that British identity and the British political tradition are in some way defined by and subservient to ethnic criteria, Parekh steers the reader away from the otherwise self-evident observation that the British constitutional tradition has been unusually successful in providing a civil and political identity which largely transcends the ethnic, cultural and regional differences within the United Kingdom. Yet surely it is by recognising and building on this accomplishment, rather than undermining it, that Britain will secure her future as a harmonious and tolerant multi-ethnic society.

The anthropologist Clifford Geertz, in discussing the emergent nationalisms of post-colonial societies, speaks of their susceptibility 'to serious disaffection based on primordial attachments'. By 'primordial', he means those forms of attachment that stem from the givens (or rather the assumed givens) of social existence: immediate kin connection and tribe, religious community, language or dialect, social customs and practices, race or skin colour—all of which are hard if not impossible for people to change or disavow, especially in thc context of a traditional society. Writing before the advent of official multiculturalism in the western world, he remarks that: 'In modern societies the lifting of such [primordial] ties to the level of political supremacy—though it has, of course, occurred, and continues to occur—has more and more come to be deplored as pathological. To an increasing degree national unity is maintained not by calls to blood and land but by a vague, intermittent, and routine allegiance to a civil state... The havoc wreaked... by those modern (or semi-modern) states that did passionately seek to become primordial rather than civil political communities... has only strengthened the reluctance publicly to advance race, language, religion and the like as bases for the definition of a terminal community.'[6]

Successful modern states (Britain among them) have sought to unite the various and often hostile groups inhabiting their territory within an effective public allegiance by sublimating the desire for primordial belonging into the commitment to an overarching structure of power which attracts loyalty with a minimum of coercive force. This is an enormous historic achievement, never entirely completed and always liable to fracture. In Britain's case, much of this work was done during the Middle Ages and early modern period, and was certainly not motivated by anything we would recognise today as ideological liberalism; yet the possibility of maintaining a liberal, consensual, tolerant public life in modern times depends in good measure upon the framework of institutions and customs established by our pre- or early modern ancestors. Perhaps official multiculturalism can best be understood as the deliberate attempt by elements within the British state to destroy this fragile and painstaking accomplishment, and to replace the traditional civil and political basis of public life in Britain with a set of competing, mutually exclusive claims of loyalty derived from primordial identities. Nothing could be better calculated to lead to the 'intolerant', 'fearful', 'insular', 'authoritarian', 'punitive', 'myopic' future that Parekh warns us of (p. 44).[7]

Not only is there a fundamental difference between constructing a sectarian political system on the basis of primordial attachments on the one hand, and, on the other, building a liberal and tolerant state based on civic and political loyalties. There is also an important and linked question as to whether our identities (primordial or civic) should be understood as something we discover or something we choose;

whether, that is, reason comes before identity, allowing us to exercise a degree of choice (however limited) about the commitments we make to society, or whether socio-cultural identity is essentially a given.

One of the many inconsistencies in the official multicultural point of view is that it is radically ambivalent in its approach to this question. Amartya Sen has observed: 'It is hardly ever presumed that, just because a person is born English, or comes from an Anglican background or a Conservative family, or has been educated in a religious school, she must inescapably think and reason within the general attitudes and beliefs of the respective groups. When, however, other cultures are considered, say in Africa or Asia, the constraints imposed by the respective cultures are taken to be much more binding and restrictive.'[8]

As Davies observes, there are basic elements of our identity which—for good or ill—we did not choose and cannot alter. Yet if we cannot select our parents, or the country of our birth, we can still exercise a high degree of choice over a multiplicity of other attachments which contribute to our sense of identity. Just as importantly, an external change in our nation's political or cultural settlement can alter the saliency of our various loyalties. Sen recalls his experience as a child in India, witnessing the sectarian violence that accompanied Partition: 'People's identities as Indians, as Asians, or as members of the human race seemed to give way—quite suddenly—to sectarian identification with Hindu, Muslim, or Sikh communities.'[9] It is hard to think of a more powerful illustration of the importance of maintaining unifying national loyalties, especially in the context of ethnically diverse modern societies.

In contrast to the reinforcement of intergroup grievances which is characteristic of official multiculturalism, a liberal and humane national policy will be guided by the fundamental consideration that '[t]he rights of minorities rest on systems that depend on the prior forging of an overriding sense of common identity'.[10] This common identity, as we have seen, need not—indeed, cannot really—be exclusive or monolithic. In Britain, the sense of common identity is a facet of society more than it is of the state; and perhaps for this reason it is seldom formally acknowledged in a public way, at least during peacetime. Rather it seems to arise informally, even idiosyncratically, from the imaginative participation of countless individuals in a broadly shared historic culture which informs, enriches, and sustains us, and which—by placing us in a tradition of ideas and practices vastly larger than our personal experiences—enables us to live not as isolated and mistrustful individuals, but as members of a society of mutually dependent citizens.

In tracing the origins of this distinctive sense of belonging, Davies finds himself drawn to the all but ubiquitous evidence of past sacrifice by which we are surrounded—the personal sacrifices of money, effort and time by which our ancestors established the vast array of our civil institutions and public amenities; and the sacrifice of young lives commemorated in war memorials in every town and village in Britain, in most of the countries of continental Europe, and indeed all over the world. 'I am an heir to all this,' he writes. 'I have no rights to this inheritance... I owe a debt of gratitude to it and to my ancestors, kin and otherwise... The appeal of a language of "rights" is neutralised by the language of gratitude, of obligation, of a real and routine awareness that I walk upon a stage I have not built.'

Here, it seems to me, Davies brings us close to the irreducible core of the matter. We did not, of course, choose the self-sacrifice of past generations. Our ancestors (kin or otherwise) chose all that, and nothing can force us to acknowledge the debt we owe them if we refuse to do so. Most of us, no doubt, have family connections with the war dead. Millions of men from all over the British Empire volunteered to fight in the two World Wars, and hundreds of thousands gave their lives. Yet even if I know that my own kith and kin are among those buried in a war grave, my connection with them now cannot be automatic. Our reaction as human beings to this overwhelming evidence of self-giving involves an act of empathy and imagination of our own—a willingness to recognise that we and the world we inhabit are the beneficiaries of past sacrifices on an unimaginable scale. From our response to this realisation arises, in large measure, both our sense of identity and our capacity to contribute to and extend—rather than to belittle, vilify and reject—our common inheritance.

Section one

1

The Report of the Equality and Human Rights Commission: *How Fair is Britain? Equality, Human Rights and Good Relations in 2010: The First Triennial Review*

> We at the Equality and Human Rights Commission come with a certain amount of baggage.
>
> Trevor Phillips[1]

Introduction

In 2010 the Equality and Human Rights Commission produced a 750 page Report entitled *How Fair is Britain? Equality, Human Rights and Good Relations in 2010: The First Triennial Review*. In the foreword to the Report, EHRC Chair Trevor Phillips describes it as the 'first comprehensive picture of its kind, enumerating the gaps between our [society's] ambitions for fairness and the actuality… a transparent and non-partisan account of where we stand now'. The Report mobilised the resources of several government departments and agencies, and of a very considerable variety of universities and independent research bodies. It is a huge effort. In its 750 pages it presents us with a most impressive array of well-attested facts and figures, usually in clear tabular form. The tables and 'boxes' in which they occasionally appear, while not particularly original, are properly referenced so that, in the best possible sense, critics (sceptics even) can subject it to objective analysis and evaluation. As such, it is a remarkably useful 'photograph' of 'where we stand now', a fine comparator for future compilers of data on our national profile. An index would have helped; and one has to be careful about missing the fact that the data sometimes refer to 'England' and sometimes to 'Britain' and sometimes (though rarely) to the 'UK'.

It would be idle to pretend, however, either that the statistical tables, boxes and other data 'speak for themselves', *or indeed that the EHRC Commissioners intended that they should.* Mr Phillips' 'baggage' surrounds the entire Report, whether in apparently slight matters such as a nuanced comment (or indeed a considered or deliberate absence of comment) on a particular datum, or in the ubiquitous presence of the EHRC's preoccupation—indeed mission—with 'challenging discrimination [and] encouraging good relations between people of different backgrounds'.[2]

This preoccupation is obvious when on pages 57-8 the Report offers an explanation of the three 'Equality Measurement Framework Indicators (EMFIs)', which it uses to classify and systematise the data.

EMFI One, 'Inequality of **outcomes**' is defined as 'the things in life that individuals and groups actually achieve'. (Achieve? A puzzling usage, as I will attempt to show.)

EMFI Two, 'Inequality of **process'**, is defined as 'inequalities in treatment through discrimination or disadvantage by other individuals and groups, including lack of dignity and respect'. Thus we have here an inequality *caused by other people.*

EMFI Three, 'Inequality of **autonomy**', is to do with 'the degree of empowerment people have to make decisions affecting their lives, how much choice and control they really have'.

EMFI One is simply a description of where we are—a *what*, a *where*, as factual as it can be: this is *what* we are, this is *where* we are: and this, indeed, is the Report's main statistical product. It is, I think, misleading to regard such descriptions as a description of 'achievement', but that is the EHRC's choice.

EMFI Two begins to explore some of the reasons *why* we (or some of us) are where we are, the language clearly asking us to look for 'discrimination' by other people and 'inequalities in treatment' (again by other people) as the reason *why*.

EMFI Three (Inequality of **autonomy**) gets us into some very difficult areas, being in essence a search for the degree of *responsibility* people have for being where they are, or for what they do or have done to deserve such a position, and what they do or do not do about being where they are. So difficult and so contentious is this question of *responsibility* that the Report ducks the whole matter, deferring such matters to a promised later Triennial Review.

The rhetoric or grammar of the Report thus invites us to see success as personal achievement (EMFI One) and inequality as failure due to discrimination by other people (EMFI Two).

As we shall see, the Report is essentially concerned with the position of various minorities, ethnic and otherwise; and on page 634 (Chapter 15, 'Improving the evidence base') we get some indications as to what will be in this promised later Review: 'autonomy', we are told, will be seen as 'a critical element in enabling people to flourish', and is defined as involving:

> self-reflection, active decision-making and having a wide range of high-quality options. Barriers to these are

conditioned expectations, passivity or coercion, and structural constraints or lack of information, advice and support.

A question phrased as 'How fair is Britain?' would seem to require, first and foremost, an answer precisely to this question of responsibility, the basis of EMFI Three. The avoidance of such an answer leaves a very large insinuation hanging in the air, i.e. that where 'unfairness' or 'inequalities in treatment' exist it is the fault of the majority society: but why should it be? And where and what are the steep and rugged pathways onto which sundry minorities are, apparently, pushed or constrained? 'If you know a better hole, go to it' comes to my Protestant British mind, as does 'If you are in a hole, why dig it deeper?' by imputing blame to everyone but yourself.

My Civitas colleague, Peter Saunders, has already analysed some of the statistical singularities of the Report; and his views are available on the Civitas website.[3] The statistics in the EHRC Report rely for their impact on the representation to the reader of disparities or inequalities in the relationship of the white majority and various minorities to sundry 'quality of life' indices such as life expectancy, wealth, education, employment. To present data in this way about the 60 million or so people who live in Great Britain, as if some injustice, some 'unfairness' *necessarily* arises out of degrees of statistical variance along a series of indices, is a large and ludicrous posture, a sufficient reason to be sceptical. One example will be enough for now: in Chapter 12 of the Report we have data on employment levels, savings and pension rights of, *inter alia*, Pakistani women and

Black Caribbean women: Pakistani women 'score' low, Black Caribbean women high. Indeed, Black Caribbean women[4] are the *only* group of women in Britain to have higher pension rights than their male equivalents (i.e. Black Caribbean men), and *higher than all men* other than white men. Black Caribbean women are more likely to be in full-time work than any other group of women. Only 24 per cent of Muslim women are at work.[5] The Report makes no useful comment on all this: sensibly, perhaps, since what do these data, *necessarily, and on their own,* tell you about the fairness, or unfairness, ***of Britain***? Does the statistical picture of Pakistani women not tell us more about Pakistan than Britain, or more properly about Pakistani *society* and British *society*, because a country is a living, cantankerous society and not just a geographical term? And 'society' can and does transcend mere national boundaries, especially these days when Lahore is but seven hours away from Bradford or Birmingham: migration is not the zero sum game it was for our ancestors who got on a sailing ship for the New World, never to return.

This fundamental conceptual error is amplified by the failure to address the matter of autonomy/responsibility—the missing EMFI Three: and together these two errors facilitate the mobilisation of an ornate language of blame, a tonality in which from the outset we see the data presented and embroidered in a definite house-style of semantics and syntax, the literary 'register' or 'refrain' of the document—its chorus. We learn, for example, from the 'outcome' data, that in England and Wales 'five times more black people than white people are imprisoned'.[6] We can perhaps just take note of this claim (surely wrong? though repeated on page 641) and move on with the Report to a consideration of some of the 'process' data (EMFI Two) connected to this statement. Here we learn that 'a large proportion of prisoners are often among the most excluded or victimised within society... Ethnic minorities can encounter racism within prisons.' Between pages 170-175 we are offered by the Report further comment on the 'ethnic' dimension of the prison population. We are told that there has been a doubling of the ethnic minority prison population in a decade, now at about 25 per cent of the prison population (such minorities being but 11 per cent of the population of England and Wales). Muslims are now about 12 per cent of the prison population (we are not told that Muslims are about two or three per cent of the general population), and that 'religious provision is made for Muslim inmates' but not so 'consistently' for other minority religions—again we are not told how many or how few Sikhs and Hindus there are in prison (actually, relatively few, proportionately very few). The absence of EMFI Three 'autonomy' data, of course, means that we do not really know, and cannot sensibly address, for example, the question of *why* black people and Muslims go to prison in such numbers: and we are left with a subtle but quite clear representation of the 'unfairness' of all this. By such 'pick and mix' of fact and comment, and very noticeable (and deliberate?) lack of comment, the Report creates a rather grim map of the unfair world through which it intends to guide us.

To round off this point: on page 435, we are confronted with an even more stark and startling fact, i.e. that the great majority (95 per cent) of those who die in work-related accidents are *men.* There is but little comment on this: and certainly no recourse to the resources of EMFI Two, or 'process' data. Yet, invoking EMFI Two, and the style and diction of pages 172-75, should we not ask whether men, as such, are being discriminated against, or shown disrespect or are being forced to live singularly unfair lives? The Report is simply not interested in 'men'.

There is a simple reason for this. However camouflaged or presented, the staple diet of the EHRC is the inequalities of outcome and of process (though not too readily of responsibility) which affect or are initiated by those racial and ethno-religious minorities of relatively recent arrival in Great Britain. The EHRC's main parent was the Commission for Racial Equality. Trevor Phillips, now Chair of the EHRC, was Chair of the Commission for Racial Equality. As a member of the Runnymede Trust, he was in part responsible for the creation of the Parekh Commission on The Future of Multi-Ethnic Britain (see below), of which indeed he was a member.

We are in the multicultural world of racial or ethnic minorities. This emphasis, this tradition, makes a great deal of sense to me. True, we are in fact given an abundance of data, an over-abundance really, dealing with the 'traditional' forms of inequalities of outcome, those of class, gender, region, i.e. our own 'indigenous' long-discussed concerns, arguments and divisions, traditionally (and to my mind satisfactorily) dealt with through the ballot box. As Philip Norton puts it: 'Weaned on the doctrine of parliamentary sovereignty, Britons have come to regard constitutional disputes as matters for resolution by political debate and not litigation.'[7] With the advent of racial or ethnic minorities, this 'weaning', this doctrine has been defined as unsatisfactory, especially for minorities: and the EHRC is one result of this, as is the way it operates and (for the purposes of this book) the literature it produces. Without ethnic minorities there would be no EHRC. The EHRC's main business is with 'Minorities' and 'Equality' and (especially) 'Rights' as they affect these minorities and, *per contra,* as they affect and are affected by the majority white British (or, for occasional ideological purposes, the English).

Necessarily, or out of choice, this summons up the world of litigation and the courts, including European courts: RIGHTS MEANS COURTS. On page 20-21 we have a list of 20 major pieces of legislation which have been passed since 1998, culminating in the Equality Act of 2010. What this means, of course, is that in this EHRC Report, as in these Acts and the numerous litigations flowing from them, the 'drama' has, as its main actors, the white majority as fixed and privileged and uneasy backdrop, contrasted with several 'new' minorities—usually (but not always) ethnic or racial or religious minorities, typically presented as the victims of some form of 'discrimination', tacit or explicit, but moving onwards under the banner of Rights.

At least one consequence follows from this. If, for example, I were to say that the relatively large proportion of black men or Muslim men in prison had something to do with a relatively high level of criminality amongst those populations, I would immediately be accused of racism and/or 'Islamophobia'. We have recently had an example of this. On 5

January 2011, Andrew Norfolk and his colleagues reported in *The Times* on the activities and conviction of gangs of men, predominantly Pakistani Muslims, who were 'grooming' young white girls for sex and prostitution. The data were taken from academic research into the criminal convictions of 56 men in 17 court cases in 13 towns in the Midlands and the North: 53 of the men were Asian, 50 of them being Muslim, and most of the victims were white. *The Times* devoted five pages, including the front page, to the story: and gave room to an article by Mohammed Shafiq of the Ramadhan Foundation, who told how he had over years been the subject of verbal and physical abuse from fellow-Muslims for trying to get the Muslim community to attend to the matter. In early January, Blackburn MP and one-time Home Secretary Jack Straw referred to 'young [Pakistani] men... fizzing and popping with testosterone... but Pakistani-heritage girls are off-limits'.[8] On 6 January 2011 *The Times* covered the experiences of Ann Cryer, former MP for Keighley, West Yorkshire, who had since 1999 been trying, with little or no success, to get both the police and Keighley's Pakistani community to attend to the cases she was getting from her constituents. Mrs Cryer told *The Times* that the dress habits of young white girls led Pakistani men to think they were 'easy meat', and that:

> Many of these men are already married or have been promised in marriage to someone they've never met, some cousin from their village in Mirpur [the region in which most Bradford-Keighley Pakistanis have their roots] who is almost certainly illiterate.

Immediately, on 7 January, Libby Brooks, in the *Guardian*, under the headline 'Our ignoble tradition of racialising crime is revived', attacked *The Times*, saying that it gave succour to the BNP, and that the claims made by *The Times* were 'dubious'. David Aaronovitch in *The Times* of 6 January 2011 wrote under the headline 'Our culture is also at fault for this awful abuse', saying that we either sexualise or repress women—or both. The Muslim Council of Britain issued a press release[9] castigating Jack Straw; and the High Commissioner for Pakistan wrote to *The Times* on 7 January saying that he and the 'Pakistani diaspora community was pained' at how 'some in Britain' welcomed the chance to 'pillory one ethnic community'. The new chief executive of Barnardo's welcomed *The Times'* breaking of the story, adding that ethnicity, while a factor, was perhaps not the key factor.[10] The government set up a national inquiry. The case is one example of how 'facts' quite quickly run into the quarrel that is multiculturalism. One of the triumphs of multiculturalism has been to confer virtue upon *ad hominem* statements. Thus in discussing the relationships between the white majority and the variety of minorities, too often the accuracy or otherwise of any particular statement or fact is measured by its source or author and not by its substance: 'Who' becomes more important than the 'What'. As with any *ad hominem* style of argument, this enables the protagonists to impute bias or prejudice to their discussants or critics, to impugn their motives and character, and—of course—to avoid the issue: the most mobilised variant of this useful irascibility is the shout of 'Islamophobia'. Racists and anti-racists all have their zealots. Multiculturalism has become a quarrel.

The EHRC and its recent Report (like so many others) springs fully-armed with concerns and quarrels about *race—colour—rights—ethnic minorities,* a medley of related burdens and issues which have exercised us only or primarily in the post-war period. These represent the main serious business of both the Commission and Report. In this, the EHRC Report is of a literary piece with conventional multicultural writing. In this book, I try to locate the Report and the EHRC within the broader context of the multicultural orthodoxies of the last 50 years or so. I am well aware of the way in which those multicultural orthodoxies have shifted and altered the nature of debate, though generally within a world of their own creation which seeks more the assertion of 'discrimination' than the proof. There is little tolerance in the multicultural world for the exegetical proposition that 'there is nothing but the text'. All texts are suspect. I will do the best I can.

In one main area the Report does deviate from its attention to ethno-race-religious issues, and this is when it discusses gender and sex—or rather those very small minorities classified as 'LGB' or 'transgender', where LGB means lesbian, gay, bi-sexual, and transgender (if I understand it correctly) means people who change their gender, either totally or partially, permanently or temporarily. For some reason, such sex-minorities (there must be a better term?) get much more mention than, for example, those unfortunate men (see above) who die at work. This perhaps relates to the other main and complementary concern of the

EHRC: the concern for *minorities, tout court*. The sex-gender minorities are indeed small: the Report states that 94 per cent of adults aged 16-59 regarded themselves as heterosexual/straight, two per cent as lesbian/gay/bisexual, and four per cent didn't know or refused to answer.[11] Yet while all minorities, *qua* minority, are equal and many indeed are called, few are chosen for the level of concern and comment devoted to LGB and transgender people. Indeed, on the EHRC's official web-site they get two 'headline' mentions—Sexual Orientation Equality and Transgender Equality. I make no comment on the data relating to these particular minorities.

The very language of the Report's analyses, and the tables and comparisons it provides, may at the outset suggest an answer to what is perhaps a self-answering question. Would any purchaser or reader of this Report anticipate the answer that Britain is indeed fair?

2

Mr Phillips's Baggage—Mislaid?

> The historical viewpoint leads to the comparative study of societies. You cannot understand or explain the major phases through which any modern Western nation has passed, or the shape it assumes today, solely in terms of its own national history. I do not mean merely that in historical reality it has interacted with the development of other societies; I mean also that the mind cannot even formulate the historical and sociological problems of this one social structure without understanding them in contrast and in comparison with other societies.
>
> C.W. Mills, *The Sociological Imagination*[1]

> What of a truth that is bounded by those mountains and is a falsehood to the world that lives beyond?
>
> Montaigne, Essays, Book 2, Chapter 12

A major defect in a Report which asks 'How Fair is Britain?' is its refusal to answer its own question. The authors are in need of attending to C. Wright Mills's insistence, above, that understanding one culture (or nation) necessitates an understanding of other cultures (or nations), as the vital comparator. This comparator may be held to include an understanding of the history of the society under examination—the past, as we know, being another country. The authors do indeed have a view of 'our' history—the complementary and equally necessary comparator—but, to repeat the point, this view does not include the crucial comparisons to which Mills points, those made with 'other societies'. Instead we are presented, as we shall see, with a rather truncated and partial 'history' of our own islands; and on the few occasions where reference is made to other countries, it is usually only to those of the EU. The rest of the world, and in particular those parts of the world from which our ethnic minorities come (or came) is all but ignored: page 89 contains what is one of the few such references to the wider world that I can find (an index would have helped—so I might be wrong). We now have ample global statistical assessments, on a variety of indices, of the 'fairness' or otherwise of most of the other 200 or so nation-states of the world. As we shall see in a later chapter, the Report makes little or no mention at all of these very valuable sources of data or of the countries they describe: they are completely absent from the concluding Chapter 15 which is called 'Improving the evidence base'!

The odd thing about a Report which asks 'How Fair is Britain?' is that it assumes it is rational and reasonable to 'answer' the question by ignoring the world of which Great Britain is a part! I shall deal with the main consequences of this failure in Chapter 10. Here I offer an illustrative example of this major flaw in this Report.

In the Summary to Chapter 6, entitled 'Life' we find the following:

> Of all of the measures reported on in this Review, life expectancy demonstrates most clearly and objectively Britain's continued development as a society. The average life expectancy has risen consistently since the Second World War; today, it exceeds by far the averages seen in our great-grandparents' lifetime. However, there remain differences between the life expectancy of different groups...[2]

I resist, for the moment, the temptation to 'deconstruct' this particular paragraph, with its idiosyncratic annexation of genealogy to history (Whose great-grandparents? Which of them were born here? Where did they come from? How did this happen?) apart from pointing out that there are no tables or data on *this* remarkable story, the story of Britain over several generations and centuries. (An aside: a couple of years ago one of my grand-daughters was doing a project on the 'Invaders of Britain'—Romans, Vikings, Normans': when I asked '*Who was being invaded* by these Romans, Vikings, Normans?' there was no answer because the question had not been put: was no one living here?) However, setting that also to one side, and turning instead to page 80 and Table 6.1.4 of Chapter 6, we get data providing 'indirect estimates of life expectancy at birth by ethnicity and gender in England, 2001'. In what follows I use where possible the Report's definitions. There are some general but not insurmountable problems with such data, but the Report's usage is sound and well-referenced.

Table 6.1.4 gives an estimate of 80.5 years life expectancy for all women born in England and of 76.0 years for all men born in England. No sub-group falls below 77.3 (Pakistani women) and 72.7 (Bangladeshi men): but on the face of it, there is undoubtedly some 'inequality' here—*in England/Britain, now.* No other country is offered as comparator: not only are we (on pages 70-71, quoted immediately above) denied any real sense of where 'we' and 'our' great grandparents come from, but also any sense of where we stand in the world now: *what would the great-grandmother of a Pakistani woman born and living and dying in Pakistan, make of the life of this great-grandchild of hers, born in and living in Britain?* How fascinating such an encounter and conversation would be! However, this question is not asked. Yet we can, very legitimately it seems to me, ignore the truncated history and the self-imposed time and geographical limits of the EHRC Report; and compare life expectancy at birth of, say, Pakistani women born in England with Pakistani women born in and living in Pakistan (and, indeed, make a similar comparison for all or any of the various Britain-born ethnic groups covered in Table 6.1.4). Complementing the Report's data with data obtained from the CIA World Fact Book for November 2010 (another well-attested source) we can show that life expectancies for some of the 'ethnic' groups are as follows:

> Indian women, England-born, 79.3 years, India-born 67.57: Indian men, England-born, 75.5, India-born 65.46:
>
> Bangladeshi women, England-born, 77.7, Bangladesh-born, 71.3: Bangladeshi men, England-born, 72.7, Bangladesh-born, 67.64:
>
> Pakistani women, England-born, 77.3, Pakistan-born, 67.5: Pakistani men, England-born 73.1, Pakistan-born, 63.84.[3]

Other differences for other ethnic minorities are even more substantial. In comparison with the general EHRC category of 'Black African' men born in Britain (life expectancy 76.1), the CIA gives life expectancy figures for male Nigerians born in Nigeria of 46.46, and for Somali men born in Somalia of 48.12. I realise that neither Nigeria nor Somalia nor Ethiopia are the same as 'Africa': the figures, though, are interesting. Lavinia Milton and Peter Aspinall have looked at the data on the 750,000 or so Africans in the UK, showing how big a part is played in their settling into 'Fair Britain' by factors such as country of birth, religion, first language, age at migration—and so on.[4] Neither here nor too readily throughout the Report is the EHRC very interested in the problems of minorities living here which they themselves might have 'imported'. Peter Saunders provides comment on the very different infant mortality rates for Pakistanis, affected by inter-cousin marriage, West Indians, who have high rates of premature births, and Bangladeshis, who have neither of these problems.[5] Returning to the data for Pakistan, we can perhaps suggest that residence in England confers very considerable benefits upon men and women of Pakistani origin. If there are a million or so Pakistani men and women born here and living here, then their stay-at-home-in-Pakistan compatriots might well envy what seems to be a ten-year increase in life expectancy for both men and women: and 10 multiplied by 1,000,000 = 10,000,000 'extra' years of Pakistani existence—a substantial gain in equality of life! No 'outcome' can be more important than that. And should it be described as 'achieved' (EMFI One) or 'conferred'?

On pages 79 and 89 of the Report we do find references to standardised mortality rates (SMRs) for people born in places like Pakistan, India and Bangladesh: by definition, of course, these are figures more *about those countries*, and not (only) about England or Britain, fair or otherwise. The Report makes no attempt to try to compare the SMRs of people born in Pakistan, but dying here, with Pakistanis both born here and dying here. The masking or denial of what might be an 'imported' problem is precisely what the EHRC's title 'How Fair is Britain?' is designed to effect.

In 'real time' in the 'real world', does it not make sense to ask, along with 'How Fair is Britain?', the question 'How Fair is Pakistan?' or 'How Fair is Bangladesh?'—the questions asked and pondered every day, presumably, by those Pakistanis and Bangladeshis who chose or choose to live here—and answered, surely and incontrovertibly, in the very fact of migration and, later, permanent settlement? In ignoring this obvious question, the Report, I suggest, loses all claim on the 'non-partisan' medal claimed for it by Trevor Phillips. To help illustrate this, I turn to another example of what seems to me to be the basic choric 'house style', the literary provenance of the document, the way in which it chooses, presents, embroiders and flourishes the data on which it relies for its sense of 'unfairness'. I repeat, here, the advice from C.W. Mills (see p. 15): and in Chapter Ten I argue that this omission of the global comparators removes the EHRC and the Report from the real world and goes a long way to undermining its moral status.

In Box 6.1.1. of Chapter 6, page 81, we are given figures for infant mortality rates, that is deaths in the first year of life per 1,000 live births. For the UK as a whole, Table 6.1.5 of Box 6.1.1 tells us that the infant mortality rate for male babies is 5.34 and 4.37 for female babies. In Box 6.1.1. a note (as opposed to a table) tells us that the infant mortality rate for Pakistani babies born in Britain is 9.8 per 1,000 live births and 4.5 for white British (these figures are not broken down by gender). From the CIA source already quoted, we know that infant mortality rates in India, Bangladesh and Pakistan are very much higher than the rates here in the UK: India, females 50.73, males 47.7; Bangladesh, females 49.94, males 55.04; Pakistan, females 67.5, males 63.84. From the EHRC Report we learn, in a rather casual way, that the combined male/female infant mortality rate for Britain-born Bangladeshis is, at 4.2, *lower* than that for the white British. No comment is made on this interesting datum. Instead the note shifts to reporting a 'concern' expressed by 'the Committee on the Elimination of Discrimination against Women', about the 'high rate of *maternal* (my emphasis) mortality among all ethnic minorities'. We are given no hard data: but these women include 'Travellers' and 'Black African female asylum-seekers', whose rate of maternal(?) mortality (the Report is a bit unclear) is 'seven times that for white women, partly due to problems in accessing maternal health care'.[6]

Again, no comment is made on the possible imported or African origins of these differences—including, of course, female circumcision or genital mutilation, not to mention the general mayhem and chaos in those countries. Difficulty in 'accessing maternal health care' on arrival in Britain may be due to a not-surprising unfamiliarity with the English language. I have no figures for maternal mortality in, for example, the Sudan or Somalia from where numbers of asylum-seeking women doubtless come. Figures for infant mortality may, however, be seen as 'proxy' data for such sad events. For Somalia the CIA source gives a rate of 107.42 per 1,000 live births, for the Sudan 72.39 per 1,000 live births. For the UK, the same source gives a figure of 4.69 per 1,000 live births:

thus for every perinatal death UK death there are 21 deaths in Somalia. In *The Times* of 17 January 2011, Dr J. Moore wrote that maternal mortality in Ethiopia was 50 times that of the UK, and infant mortality 25 times that of the UK. The Ethiopian population had increased from 40 million in 1985 to 80 million by 2010—trouble, and unfair, indeed. *The Times* for 15 December 2010 reports that in the Southern Sudan 93 per cent of the population has no access to sanitation, there are ten midwives for about 10,000,000 people, a woman giving birth has a 1:50 chance of dying and all educated people who might have become doctors and midwives have fled the country, no doubt fleeing the civil war which has been threatening now for decades.

The only comment that the EHRC Report makes on the problems of these black African women—the reference to 'problems of accessing maternal health care'—puts at least part of the blame on Britain and totally ignores what life is like in their country of origin. Naturally, at no point are we told that the 'obvious solution', the 'fair' solution, for all these human beings is to take care to be born in Britain! ***No one who comes to the UK from countries like Somalia or the Sudan, or having come here stays and gives birth, is worse off than where they come from.*** As I said above, only very occasionally does the EHRC make any comment about other countries, the countries from which ethnic minorities come or came.

A couple of years ago, I was discussing with a Pakistani friend the conditions surrounding the recent birth of his son, Mohammed, born in the Royal Victoria Infirmary in Newcastle upon Tyne. Both parents are Pakistan-born Pakistani citizens. Baby Mohammed's mother (his father's cousin) had had two previous miscarriages: and Mohammed's birth was difficult, requiring substantial pre-natal care and the best part of a year of intensive post-natal care (all free, of course). My granddaughter was born at about the same time, so we had a 'theme' in common. My friend, Mohammed's father, was a medical doctor, undergoing post-graduate training in the UK. As men do at such times, we discussed the then available facts and figures of perinatal morbidity and mortality. These did not differ very much from the more up-to-date figures which are now to be found, above, and in the EHRC Report.

My Pakistani friend knew, from personal experience, what his world was like and how it compared with Britain. Most unwillingly, and only because his medical course was over and his visa therefore invalid, he and his family were forced to return to Pakistan. He—a qualified doctor—had been working here as a night-time guard on a building site. Still, he did not want to go to work at his profession in Pakistan: 'Pakistan', he said, 'is the worst country in the world'. Britain, though, had been more than fair to him and to his wife and to his child.

Section Two

3

Of Human Rights and Human Equality

> The concepts of Equality and Diversity must be driven through the Government machinery at national and regional levels… There must be a sustained and fearless attack on all forms of racial injustice... street racism and violent racism… but also institutional racism… Attention must be paid to anti-black racism, anti-Muslim racism, anti-gypsy racism, anti-Irish racism, anti-semitism, and so on.
>
> Bikhu Parekh, *The Future of Multi-Ethnic Britain* [1]

From each according to his ability? To each according to their need?

Fluently and ubiquitously present in the EHRC Report and in the general canon of multicultural writing from which it derives are notions of 'Rights' and 'Equality'. The doctrine of 'Rights' is one of the most alluring and elusive creeds of political theory, making both vivid and semi-spectral appearances throughout the EHRC Report—and in this book, therefore. The Report carries within itself a generously promiscuous understanding of such matters, an understanding not too readily subsumed, it seems to me, under the more traditional and restricted one of 'from each according to his ability, unto each according to his needs'. As we shall see, little is said of 'Obligations' or 'Duties' or 'Responsibilities'—or, and more importantly in my mind, Gratitude. Rather like the BBC, the EHRC may be seen as being part of a distinctive post-war (post-60s, really) top-down cultural Establishment, a bit of New Labour which seems set to survive the overall collapse of that enterprise. All of the current Commissioners were appointed under Labour, before the 2010 General Election. Of the 14 Commissioners, seven have clear Labour and Trade Union loyalties and careers, and one a Liberal commitment. The EHRC Report expresses the distinctive set of rhetorical or literary tropes favoured by this Establishment, symbolised philosophically by the word 'RIGHTS' and legislatively by the Human Rights Act and the Equality Act. The Report endeavours to give substantive (and often statistical meaning) to these inherently abstract ideas.

After a few preliminary words on 'Rights', 'Equality' (and, in one distinctive EHRC sense, on 'Obligations') I will locate the EHRC within this post-war/post-60s culture, paying particular attention to two significant events, the Parekh Commission's *Report on The Future of Multi-Ethnic Britain*, 2000; and the Macpherson Inquiry, 1997/9, into the death in London in 1993 of the black teenager Stephen Lawrence. Linking these foundational texts of multiculturalism, and a most influential player in the story, is Trevor Phillips, current Chair (*sic*) of the EHRC, already quoted above as saying that 'we [at] the EHRC come with a certain amount of baggage'.[2] Mr Phillips seems to have been on every Commission producing this baggage: he is, if he doesn't mind me saying so, the baggage-master. Indeed, Mr Phillips, as head of the Runnymede Trust, was participant in the early forms and flourishings of multiculturalism, to which I will also refer.

Of Rights (and obligations?)

> Some writers have so confounded society with government as to leave little or no distinction between them: they are not only different, but have different origins. Society is produced by our wants, and government by our wickedness; the former promotes our happiness positively by uniting our affections, the latter negatively by restraining our vices. The one encourages intercourse, the other creates distinctions. The first is a patron, the last a punisher. (Thomas Paine, *Common Sense*, 1776[3])

'We are born free and equal', says an EHRC video (3 November 2010). Tom Paine would have approved (I think). The Equality and Human Rights Commission, as its official title demonstrates, exists to try to give some kind of operational substance to at least two of the traditional concerns of political thought, the concern for 'equality' and the concern for 'human rights': it is necessary to separate these words 'human' and 'rights', as however glibly they now talk and walk hand in hand they are not intrinsically related. Either one of these, on its own, has baffled the best of our political philosophers: it has proved almost impossible, for example, to confer a meaning on 'rights' when they are located in 'humans', pure and simple, for there is no limit to the human appetite: and if humans have, *qua* human, rights, then no human authority can be licensed to broaden or limit them: a right is anything that I want and everything I should have: and equal human rights consist in your having the right to anything that I might have or that you might want—or vice versa. While all rights may be equal, some (as the EHRC Report makes abundantly clear) are more equal than others. Where, for example are my rights when

Mr Cameron, having promised me that he would repeal the Human Rights Act (which he described as 'a glaring example of what is going wrong in our society'), exercises his right to change his mind? When a foreign-born murderer cannot be deported to his country of birth because such deportation contradicts his human rights, where are the rights of the woman made a widow by the murderer?[4] In the chaos of this creative immunity to the complexity of human things, where and what is the EHRC? Is it Government or Society? In Paine's terms, does it exist because of our wickedness or because of our happiness? Does it promote intercourse or distinction? Is it patron or punisher?

There is a philosopher to whom we can turn for some answer to these questions.

> *Afin donc que ce pacte sociale ne soit pas un vain formulaire, il renferme facilement cet engagement, que seul peut donner de la force aux autres, que quoiconque refusera d'obeir a la volonte generale, y sera contraint par tout les corps : ce que ne signifie autre chose sinon qu'on le forcera d'etre libre : car telle est la condition qui, donnant chaque citoyen a la patrie, le garantit de toute dependance personelle, condition qui fait l'artifice et le jeu de la machine politique, et qui seul rende legitimes les engagements civils, lesquels, sans cela, seroient absurdes, tyranniques, et sujets aux plus enormes abus.*

> In order that the social contract should be something other than an empty formula, it must be understood to contain this commitment (which alone gives force to all the others) that whoever refuses to obey the general will, will then be forced to be free: for such is the situation whereby, when each person is given to the nation, he is then protected against any personal subordination or dependency, and against the artifice and frivolity of

> politics, so that in this way alone are his contractual obligations rendered legitimate, which would otherwise be absurd, tyrannical and liable to the greatest abuse.[5]

What we have in Britain at the moment is not the 'tyranny of the majority' predicted by de Tocqueville. The EHRC is clearly not 'the government', and indeed is insistent upon its independence of governments. Equally clearly, it is not 'just another' sectional bit of civil or voluntary society, with limited purposes and (usually) limited finance. It is most certainly not The People. It is more like a resurrected Parliament of Saints. The EHRC has been well-funded, and exists to blanket society as a whole with its own moralising purpose. We are told by one of the Commission's intellectual parents that: 'If Britain is to flourish as a community of citizens and communities, its political leaders should shape, and not pander to, public opinion on issues relating to race and diversity.'[6] Here, multiculturalism comes as close as anything can to Rousseau's conception of 'La Volonté Generale', 'The General Will', by which he meant an overriding moral and moralising sense of what people *should* want to do even if (or especially if) they don't, actually, either want to do it or intend to do it. When such people are unable to see what is in their own and society's best interests, then being forced (by 'the general will') to be free is indeed a form of liberation and progress, defined and conferred for and on us—by the EHRC. Then, and only then, will Britain 'flourish': Equal, Human, Right.

The EHRC seeks to promote, and if necessary to impose, *as its and our only obligation,* a generalised public subscription to the canonisation of 'rights'. To create a 'General Will to Rights' is the task entered into and pursued by the very public and potent busy-ness of the official Guardians of Rights such as, prototypically, the EHRC. Step by step, case by minatory case, the public is, by the EHRC and its attendant satrapies, brought to shoulder a peculiar indefectible obligation, an obligation to spread and respect 'rights' as widely and as deeply and as emphatically and as empathetically as possible. By degrees, ordinary decent (or obsequious?) human beings, as well as their more formal and official representatives, are brought to believe that it is their business, their obligation, to ensure that there is a general acceptance, 'une volonté generale', of a duty to live in a world of rights.

The assiduous proclamation and conferment of rights becomes an anxious politeness, a rights-respecting gift proffered with determination—as when, for example, the owners of the Early Learning Centre's Happy Land Goosefeather Farm at their own initiative removed, from its toy farm-set, the pig—lest its presence offend Muslims. The 'oink' of the pig was unfortunately (perhaps) left on the audio-panel which accompanied the farm-set, an outcome which would have amused the author of *Animal Farm*. Muslim mother Safiyyah, seemingly less sensitive about her rights than many, and perhaps aware that rights could not so easily be individualised, said 'it doesn't bother me'.[7] On the same day as the *Sun* carried this rather trivial story, the *Telegraph* carried the more serious account of the protection of gay rights by the dismissal of a Christian paediatrician who, having a religious belief, had refused to take part in the placement of adoptive children in gay households.[8] On the evening of the same day both radio and television carried the story of several Muslim men whose incarceration in Guantanamo Bay had transgressed their (human) rights and who could therefore expect millions of pounds in compensation, it being my right to contribute to this payment. On 19 November 2010 the *Daily Telegraph*, under the headline 'Race not the basis for stop and search', reported that plans to allow police to use ethnicity to stop and search people have been dropped. Draft Home Office guidance on how stop-and-search powers could be used included a clause allowing officers to take race into account when responding to 'a specific threat or incident'. This clause had been removed from the finalised guidelines following pressure from the EHRC. The new guidance states, helpfully, that officers 'must take care not to discriminate unlawfully' against 'anyone on the grounds of race, sex or religious beliefs'. Throughout this whole period, the EHRC was using its statutory powers to force a change in the membership criteria of the BNP, to force it to be free of its restriction of party membership to white people, a restriction which is a denial of the rights of both white people and those black and brown people who might wish to join the BNP or indeed of those black and brown people who might wish to refuse to join the BNP. The case is currently with the courts. The EHRC cannot simply sit in London amiably urging human rights upon us all: it cannot, in isolation, and without the force of law, create a culture of rights. The will to rights must be social and governmental, optional and compulsory, judicial and administrative, the shared ubiquitous morality of the nation, the General Will. At every level—toy pigs, gay adoption, Guantanamo Bay, stop and search, the BNP—the assiduous proclamation of rights is forcing recalcitrant citizens to realise that they *must* be free—or else.

4

The Origins of the Equality and Human Rights Commission

The Commission came into legal existence in 2006, when the Equality Act of the same year amalgamated the Commission for Racial Equality, the Equal Opportunities Commission and the Disability Rights Commission. It began work in October 2007. The Labour government of 1997-2010 had passed and driven forward the Human Rights Act, giving formal British subscription to the European Convention on Human Rights. The Equality Act of 2010, currently under review (perhaps), both protected and extended the duties of the EHRC and its status as one of three publicly funded bodies (the other two being the Electoral Commission and the BBC) which have a statutory guarantee of independence from the government. The EHRC survived the Coalition government's 2010 'cull' of quangoes, although the new Government both cut back its budget and promises a 'radical' review of its functions.[1] Mr Trevor Phillips, a broadcaster, an ex-member of the London Assembly, and since 2003 head of the Commission for Racial Equality, is Chair (*sic*) of the EHRC. Labour peer Baroness Prosser of Battersea is his deputy. The 12 current Commissioners were all appointed or re-appointed during the dying days of the Labour governments of 1997-2010, that is before the General Election of 2010 and the arrival of the Coalition government. The Conservative Party Manifesto included a promise to repeal the Equality Act of 2010.

At the time of writing, there is some doubt about what is to happen, though if *Pink News*[2] is anything to go by, far from repeal, the Minister in charge of 'equalities' at the Home Office, Liberal Democrat Lynne Featherstone, intends to provide gay people with the right to have religious readings, music etc. at their ceremonies. Home Secretary Theresa May is, apparently, not so minded. It would seem that while the budget of the EHRC has been cut back, its ambitions have not.

Trevor Phillips, currently in charge of the EHRC, links several of the major 'events' lying behind the advent of the EHRC and the associated legislation. He is an omnipresent figure in the elaboration of government-sponsored multiculturalism; and his 2008 speech at Leeds Social Sciences Institute, to which I will on occasion refer, provides a fine summary of the operational ideology of his Commission. Together with people and events, we have other 'seminal moments', of which two are probably the most important: (1) the publication of the Parekh Report, 'The Future of Multi-Ethnic Britain, 2000', by a Commission of which Lord Parekh was Chair (and of which Trevor Phillips was a member); and (2) the publication of the Macpherson Report in February 1999 on the death of the black teenager Stephen Lawrence.[3] These two documents and related events can be read together as foundational texts of multiculturalism, with its particular versions of Rights and Equalities. The Parekh Report was, for example, described as 'the most important contribution to the national debate on racial discrimination for many years'.[4] During the course of this long national debate, two major strands of contemporary 'New Labour' multiculturalism had begun to come together to form a rather strange political alliance. On the one hand, there were the in-coming minorities, many of them initially coming from lands which had been part of the British Empire. To their own direct or familial experience of colonialism they added a self-interested zeal so to re-write the terms of their own various settlements here that large reparation would be exacted as a condition of taking citizenship of this small island nation, once empire. To most British people, relatively untouched by the imperial exploit (the Empire had always been 'somewhere else', i.e. overseas[5]), this conflation of national quotidian habits with the imperial story was, and remains, more than a little puzzling. Contrary to Parekh[6] our 'common identity' was not 'forged' though our imperial and colonial role. However, for a large element of indigenous British political life, the always-about-to-be-redundant ultra-Left, the new minorities and their causes came to represent a surrogacy or proxy for the proletariat, which, having failed to live up to Marxist expectations, could now be reinvented in the proletarian cause as 'minorities' and as such supported in its, or their, long march though the institutions of the once-imperial always-capitalist state. It helped, of course, that on the world stage these minorities were, in fact, anything but minority: they were the workers of the world come to plant the Red Flag of liberty on this old and sour and disappointed soil, a rejuvenant presence indeed.

This new 'anti-racial' alliance was not content merely to disparage and exorcise the Empire. It had also to re-write, and exorcise, our national story. In my book of 2007, *Bonfires on the Ice*,[7] I detail some of the contours of this effort: thus a glossy pamphlet published jointly by the Foreign and Commonwealth Office, the Home Office, and MCBDirect has, in a section called 'Muslim Roots in British Soil', reference to a brooch dated to the reign of King Offa and a reference to Muslims in the *Canterbury Tales*, both presented as the beginnings of 'our Muslim story'.[8] In the same publication, the then Foreign Secretary Jack Straw assures us that 'Islam is part of our past and our present; in all fields of human endeavour it has helped to forge modern Europe'.[9] King Offa and Chaucer aside, one of the oddest symbols of the early multi-culturalism is the Runnymede Trust, named after the 1215 events involving King John and his barons. The Runnymede Trust has been highly influential in British race relations/multicultural politics; and indeed set up the Parekh Commission whose Report has been so authoritative. It is difficult to imagine what the barons of 1215 would make of this symbolic annexation of their efforts and of the traditions which grew out of them. Little more than barely-polite guffaws greeted the Trust's 2009 report *Who Cares about the White Working Class?* when it assured us that while white men and women were indeed discriminated against it was not—much, no doubt, to their delight and relief—because they were white!

Attendant upon the work and publications of these various bodies came an irruption of *religion* into our national life, 'religion' that is in the form of Islamist bombs (in New York and London) and in the form of murders of, and threats to the lives of sundry novelists, cartoonists and politicians. These events radically altered the tone and future of 'multi-ethnic' Britain:

and gave rise to particular problems for the traditionally secular Left.

Few commentators or academics had predicted the re-appearance of *religion* as a contender for space in our society, it generally being held by sociologists and others that 'secularism' and 'the West' went hand in hand. Few students wanted to study religion; little money was available for research; and the staffs of university religious studies or theology departments were regarded as eccentric pedlars of obscure and irrelevant things. Bombs and murders changed all that. The EHRC and related governmental institutions have come to realise that religion is 'relevant' and that some forms of 'Islam' are a problem. At the time of writing, 'religion', in particular the religion of the Middle East, is causing very public anxiety in British universities, the head of one highly prestigious university college, the LSE, being forced to resign because of the Libyan version of it. The state security services deploy most of their staff on matters to do with Islam; and a now-depleted government 'Prevent' programme sought to deal with 'the Muslim problem' through extensive 'community' programmes. My 2010 book for Civitas, *A New Inquisition*,[10] deals with the problem of 'religious hatred', a new entrant in the legal world of wrongs and rights; and my 2009 book for the Social Affairs Unit *In Search of the Moderate Muslim*[11] makes a contribution to the debates we have been having about the presence and behaviour of Muslims in the UK and the wider world. Such writings are of course but a tiny bit of what is published by and about Muslims (in particular) and religion in general. It should be said that Muslims or Islam have, as Mr Straw said, a distinctive part in the drama of British multiculturalism, a fact obscured by the deployment of the 'Equality' thesis. The multicultural world, weaned on Equality, force-fed on Rights, has to assume that all cultures are equal, equal in value, equal in basic norms, in effect the same—which they clearly are not.

I turn now to one of the major scriptures of multiculturalism and of the Equality and Human Rights Commission, the Report of the Commission on the Future of Multi-Ethnic Britain, named after its Chair (*sic*) Lord (Bhikhu) Parekh.

5

Lord Parekh and his Report

The proper name of the 400 page Parekh Report is *The Future of Multi-Ethnic Britain*, published in 2000. The Runnymede Trust ('devoted to the cause of promoting racial justice in Britain') commissioned the Report and expected the Commissioners to:

> Analyse the current state of multi-ethnic Britain and to propose ways of countering racial discrimination and disadvantage and making Britain a confident and vibrant multicultural society at ease with its rich diversity'.[1]

The Commission has been described as 'the most important contribution to the national debate on racial discrimination for many years [and it] led to the reform of Britain's social, cultural and political institutions',[2] an opinion offered on the occasion of a decennial commemorative lecture at the LSE. The Chair of the Commission, Bhikhu Parekh, was raised to the peerage in the year of the Report's publication.

Given the nature of its task, it is clearly not surprising that Britain—a Britain radically re-configured, de-constructed, re-constructed even—is the main geographical focus of the Parekh Report. In this it prefigures the 2010 EHRC Report. It might seem both churlish and stupid to make something of this again: yet this strangely limited geographical focus becomes, as we shall see, part of the unquestioned house-style of multiculturalism, rather like one of those travel brochures bruiting the delights of one place as if none of the others existed. This, of course, might not matter—except for the fact that 'travel'—

mental travel at least—between different places is precisely what multiculturalism is—or should be—all about. Like its sundry offspring, the Parekh Report is almost completely unwilling to raise its eyes beyond the shores of our narrow little island. One small island is written onto the history of the world as if the very world which now feeds its scions into it does not exist—but then neither, after Parekh and his Commissioners are finished, does Britain.

Chapter Two of the Parekh Report, called 'Rethinking the national story', starts with one of many rather odd literary devices, the presentation of a series of 'Submissions' or 'Responses' made to the Commission by correspondents or witnesses. These seem to be included so as to enable Parekh to say things about which a degree of reticence might have otherwise been called for. In a submission on page 14 we learn that:

> The future of Britain lies in the hands of descendants of slave owner and slaves, of indentured labourers, of feudal landlords and serfs, of industrialists and factory workers, of lairds and crofters, of refugees and asylum seekers.

Lest this be taken as mere banality, the main text of this chapter ends with what is a standard trope of multicultural writing, the non-existence of Britain:

> First, Britain is not and never has been the unified conflict-free land of popular imagination. There is no single white majority.[3]

This leads on to Chapter 3, Identities in Transition, one of the shortest in the Report. This starts with yet another submission or response to the Commission, in which Britain is further disestablished—by a Scot!

> The young participants, school and college pupils, stated that they were proud to be Scottish. 'I want to be Scots not English. I want to be Scottish and British, but not if people assume that being British means being English. Too often people talk about England when they mean Britain and they forget about Scotland'. But they also asked a number of pointed questions. Why should it be a problem to be Scottish, born in England, of French nationality and part Indian? Or to be from the North-East of England, although born in Scotland?... How late it is, how late to be asking these questions.[4]

After a slight embarrassment—the respondents clearly felt that the Scottish nation existed—the writer of this submission felt free to move on to a version of the 'We-are-a-Nation-of-Immigrants' theme: and Chapter 3, 'Identities in Transition', gives us (1) African-Caribbean communities, (2) 'Asian' communities, (3) Irish communities, (4) Jewish communities, (5) Gypsy and Traveller communities. Parekh notes that official statistics are often of limited use—'they do not include East Europeans, since most define themselves as white';[5] and concludes:

> The shifting complexities and uncertainties outlined above illustrate that there are few stable patterns from which future projections can be made: differences in origin and development will continue to shape attitudes towards wider integration. However, all the people discussed are enmeshed in and having an impact on life around them. Like every other element in the social mix, they are busy negotiating place and space within a rapidly changing larger whole.[6]

This is enormously helpful: but the 'travel brochure' analogy I referred to earlier breaks down because the Parekh Report, like its various successors, advertises and emphasises not delights but miseries: on its presentation, Britain becomes a place not to go to. So, early on in Parekh, in a summary of several longer chapters, we get the following musing on the future of Britain, seen as in 'urgent need of re-imagining itself'.[7] Eight futures await, we are told, should we turn our faces from multiculturalism: we will become static (as opposed to dynamic), intolerant (as opposed to cosmopolitan), fearful (as opposed to generous), insular (as opposed to internationalist), authoritarian (as opposed to democratic), introspective (as opposed to outward-looking), punitive (as opposed to inclusive), myopic (as opposed to far-sighted). Parekh assures us that 'it is the second term in each of these pairings that evokes the kind of Britain that is proposed in this Report'.[8] No doubt this is all meant to be helpful and kind—to assist native-born Brits like me to be free of our cultural detritus: yet whether any of this is *true* or not is surely a matter of some concern. Were we, after all our history, indeed set to become static, fearful, insular, intolerant, authoritarian and punitive before the arrival of various ethnic minorities and the redemptive and reparative awareness of a wider world that they conferred upon us? Anyway, we now know, as Lord Parekh tells us, that 'England, Scotland and Wales are multi-ethnic, multi-faith, multicultural, multi-community societies'.[9]

In the film *The Sheepman*, the hero Glenn Ford wishes to dramatise the fact that he *has arrived*, with his sheep, in a cattle-ranching town, and that he is determined to stay and herd sheep. Whatever resistance there might be, he and his sheep will change things for the better—as well as to his benefit. To make his point, he struts into the local bar, smoking a cigar and with his hat at a rakish angle. Up to the bar he goes, and says to the bartender: '*Who is the toughest man in town?* The bartender indicates a huge man, standing at the end of the bar, tucking into a great pile of mashed potatoes. Glenn Ford swaggers over to him, takes the cigar out of his mouth and shoves it into the toughest-man-in-town's pile of potatoes. Huge insult, huge fight. Glenn Ford wins. Eventually what was a mere cow town becomes a sheep town as well: Glenn Ford gets the girl, the cowboys get sheep.

What is being promulgated in Parekh and its descendant writings seems to me to be an officially-sanctioned insult-ability of the British, though perhaps offered more in the expectation of a kind of secular General Confession than a fight. Indeed, on page 279 we get (in yet another submission or response) precisely that:

> Racism is often portrayed as though it is something like a disease which can be cured... [Racist beliefs] are reinforced in so many ways in white people, from the cradle... It is not a question of curing me, but of me acknowledging my racism and taking personal responsibility for operating in a non-racist way personally and encouraging organisations and institutions in which I have an influence to do the same.

This has the tone of the Anglican General Confession which I say at least every Sunday! (I do, of course make my confession to God, merely.) The Parekh text continues: on page 24 we learn that we (the British) are 'tempted to look back, nostalgically, to past glories' and that our failure to re-examine our imperial history is 'an unmitigated disaster'.[10] There seems little boundary to (or humour about) these insults: on page 19 we learn that for centuries 'English kings were vassals of French kings and not, as myth has it, the reverse'. Shakespeare clearly owes Parekh, and me, an apology. Page 57 presents us with another submission to the Commission, in which the Last Night at the Proms, the singing of Rule Britannia and remembering World War Two are censured ('Britain seems incapable of shaking off its imperialist identity') and are adduced as proof that 'Britain has never understood itself'. The submission is worth quoting in full—as Parekh obviously felt that it was:

> The Rule Britannia mindset, given full-blown expression at the Last Night of the Proms and until recently at the start of programming each day on BBC Radio 4, is a major part of the problem of Britain. In the same way that it continues to fight the Second World War... Britain seems incapable of shaking off its imperialist identity. The Brits do appear to believe that 'Britons never, never, never shall be slaves... [But] it is impossible to colonise three fifths of the world... without enslaving oneself. Our problem has been that Britain has never understood itself and has steadfastly refused to see and understand itself through the prism of our experience of it, here and in its coloniser mode.[11]

So—I am a slave! Worse, it is it seems wrong for me to want not to be a slave! From this dreadful fate we are to be rescued by (and can only be rescued by) ethnic minorities: and in order to pre-empt scepticism about the salvific potency of such a small addition to our gene pool or to our cultural resource, we are provided on page 223 with a reassurance, another 'submission':

> The proportion of ethnic minority electors as compared to the total electorate is tiny. But so is the thumb as a physical proportion of your body. But try picking up your pen without the aid of your thumb. It is its strategic position that gives it a disproportionate importance.[12]

Seldom can so many have had their immortal souls and earthly lives saved by so inelegant a digit. To back up the strategic and salvific thumb, Parekh provides 131 recommendations covering every aspect of life in multi-ethnic Britain,[13] and leaves a legacy of over 100 separate pieces of legislation—including the EHRC and its Report. Before getting back to that, we have to consider the other natural parent of Mr Phillips and the EHRC, the report of the Stephen Lawrence Inquiry, usually known as the Macpherson Report, leaving Parekh with this thought: 'Europe got over the loss of its colonies much more quickly than the colonies got over their loss of Europe.'[14]

6

The Macpherson Report

Lord Parekh made much of the story of the murder of Stephen Lawrence and of the Report by Sir William Macpherson. On the night of 22 April 1993 a young black man, Stephen Lawrence, was murdered in East London by (it would seem) a gang of white youths, though no one has been found guilty of the murder. For a variety of reasons, this one murder led to a several inquiries and a full-scale Public Inquiry which reported in 1999 as the Stephen Lawrence Inquiry, Command Paper Cm 4262. It also led to films, plays, television dramas—an extraordinary prolonged effusion, much of it motivated by the apparent failure of the criminal justice system to find and bring Stephen Lawrence's killers to trial. Mrs Lawrence told the initial inquest that 'our crime is living in a country where the justice system supports racist murders against innocent people'.[1] Stephen Lawrence's parents were both awarded the OBE for their services to the community. Stephen Lawrence is one of the '100 Great Black Britons' listed on the website of that name (so incidentally is Trevor Phillips).[2] The murder of Stephen Lawrence and the long travail of the Macpherson Inquiry and Report were probably the most potent and weighty influences on British policing in the last 30 years. This is so partly because it co-incided with the great out-put of legislation and regulation associated with various equality and human rights ambitions of the Labour government—which indeed set up the

Lawrence Inquiry. Rarely can the piteous death of one young man have had such momentous consequences.

As I have said, so great and vocal was the ostensible public interest in the case that in 1997 New Labour Home Secretary Jack Straw appointed Sir William Macpherson to head an Inquiry into Stephen Lawrence's death. In February 2009 Mr Straw, in a speech at Westminster Hall, quoted Sir William's words that the murder was 'simply and solely and unequivocally motivated by racism', described the murder and Macpherson's report as 'a landmark... which challenged us all... a defining moment in our history, a test of moral leadership, one which has profoundly changed the character of our society'.[3] A Home Office research study of 2005 described the Report as 'one of the most significant events in British policing in the last decade'.[4] This study was in itself an addition to the extraordinary range of consequences resulting from the murder of one young man in the East End of London. Thus, for example, the authors of the research paper state that they had a 'Lawrence Steering Group' whose members included not only the then Home Secretary Charles Clarke but also the mother of the murdered Stephen—and, perhaps inevitably, Trevor Phillips, then running the CRE.

The Macpherson Inquiry was marked by several unusual comments, features and results: for example, in a rather non-judicial manner, Sir William Macpherson described the (unidentified) gang of white youths who killed Stephen Lawrence as 'a group of murderers... bent on violence... cowards... the sort [who] rarely act on their own'.[5] At the time when he made that comment, Sir William Macpherson had neither met these 'cowards' nor indeed had any such cowards been identified and arrested, never mind convicted, even though the 'double jeopardy' prohibition of more than one trial for the same charge was later removed in order to facilitate the continuing activities of the police and the CPS. This is yet another example of the way in which the pursuit of multi-cultural 'rights' has seen the dismantling of various legal safeguards built up over centuries.[6] My late colleague Norman Dennis's book shows how Sir William got caught up in the missionary zeal of the multiculturalists.[7]

To return to Macpherson: Sir William said:

> We believe that the immediate impact of the Inquiry has brought forcibly before the public the justifiable complaints of Mr and Mrs Lawrence and the hitherto underplayed dissatisfaction and unhappiness of ethnic minorities, both locally and all over the country, in connection with this and other cases, as to their treatment by police'.[8]

Following this line of thought, Sir William came up with what was to be his major contribution to the language of multiculturalism, the epithet 'institutional racism', an epithet visited not just upon the Metropolitan Police but gradually on all police forces—and steadily upon all public services and the nation in general. In this, Macpherson was aware that Lord Scarman, who had earlier conducted the inquiry into the troubles in Brixton, had said 'institutional racism does not exist in Britain'[9] and that he and others had warned about the danger that the word 'racism' might become a 'rhetorical weapon'.[10]

Nevertheless, Sir William produced and applied his very influential definition:

> Institutional racism is the collective failure of an organisation to provide an appropriate and professional service to people because of their colour, culture or ethnic origin. It can be seen or detected in processes, attitudes and behaviour which amount to discrimination through unwitting prejudice, ignorance, thoughtlessness and racist stereotyping which disadvantage minority ethnic people.[11]

Both at the time, and later, and indeed now, this was a concept of problematic provenance and of problematic empirical referent. Indeed, Macpherson himself said that his definition did 'not produce a definition cast in stone, or a final answer to the question'.[12] Neither was Macpherson's discovery grounded in such evidence as he heard—in what was, after all, an inquiry into the behaviour of the Metropolitan Police. Thus he said: 'We have not heard evidence of overt racism or discrimination, unless it can be said that the use of inappropriate expressions such as "coloured" or "negro" fall into this category.'[13]

This did not stop Macpherson: and certainly not Parekh, who chose to regard the Macpherson Report as describing the reality of life in 'the policies and procedures of many public bodies',[14] thus contributing to the extension of 'institutional racism' into ever broader and broader ranges of the public services. Earlier, Dr Robin Oakley giving evidence to the Inquiry, and in what Macpherson referred to as a 'helpful note', said that: 'institutional racism was pervasive throughout the culture and institutions of British society, it is in no way specific to the police service'.[15] Parekh complicated things even more by adding to Macpherson's word-pictures of life in our public services such subtleties as 'organisational body language':

> In all professional relationships a fundamental principle is that an official should show respect. But whether respect is indeed shown rests on the perceptions of members of the public, not on those of the official. Communication of respect depends on a range of non-verbal behaviours as well as, and often instead of, on words alone—body language, gesture, facial expression, physical closeness or distance, the spatial surroundings and so on—all this adds to the complexity. Further increasing the complexity is the fact that every piece of communication (and miscommunication) is part of a history, and is interpreted in the light of past experience, and of conflicting memories. There is such a thing as organisational body language, as well as personal body language.[16]

In many societies, of course, 'respect' is demanded by an official of the supplicant: and it is difficult to know how or what the average policeman (or any other public servant), would make of or do about, for example, the 'institutional racism' or 'organisational body language' of his police force, though it is clear from even the polite language of the document referred to above that many a constable was in some difficulty.[17]

The main significance of Macpherson's 'institutional racism' and of Parekh's persistent use of it as applicable to the public services in general, is that the term is employable not in spite of its imprecision but because of it. Under the shelter of its very useful imprecision, and when one is setting off virtuously on the track of the ubiquitous 'racism' of the police and the public sector in general, it becomes respectable to ignore any suggestion of the need for a specific empirical referent. The 'institution' is something other than the people employed in it: and its 'racism' is neither embodied (nor embody-able) in nor refuted (or refute-able) by them, any more by word than by deed. Persons calling for some caution in the use of the term can themselves be advised to consider that their very caution is simply a denial, and may legitimately be adduced as proof of the contagious subtlety of the very demoniacal urge that is being pursued. The confessional urge spread, too, to Scotland:

> [Scotland's Lord Advocate, said that] The starting point for all of us in response to the Macpherson report should be one of diligent self-assessment... If there is discrimination, it is our duty as prosecutors to identify the difficulty and remedy the situation as far as possible. Failure to do so by us ignores the fact that Scottish society is multicultural and that Scotland is the richer because of the varied ethnic origins of her citizens... The challenge of the Lawrence Inquiry is one for all of us at a personal and professional level.[18]

There is, then, a large consequence of the now-quotidian lustration of our public services with the disinfectant salve of 'institutional racism'. No mere empirical 'defence' can be possible, if only because recourse to defence is in itself proof that there is something rotten in the public service state. Conversely, even the slightest complaint made by (or on behalf of) those who are the 'victims' of, say, institutional racism and racist and stigma-inducing 'organisational body language', must be either automatically assumed to be 'true' or seen at the very least as calling for a major inquiry or inquest—of the sort, indeed, that gave us the Macpherson Report. The numerous tables and graphs presented to us in the EHRC's Report are not simply a matter of attending to a possible 'victim': they are missionary eschatology in tabular form, proffered rites of redemption made by the minorities on behalf of the majority, as well as for themselves. It is by Lord Parekh's Thumb (p. 47) that we are saved.

7

Parekh + Macpherson = the Equality and Human Rights Commission: The Conscience of the Nation—or the Baggage of the Nation?

On 19 January 2009 Trevor Phillips's speech provided the basic theology of the coming together of Macpherson and Parekh, the quintessential *leitmotiv* of multiculturalism, of the EHRC and of the 2010 Report *How Fair is Britain?* His speech was entitled: 'Institutions must catch up with the public on race issues'—the General Will exemplified—and took place to mark the tenth anniversary of the Stephen Lawrence Inquiry. Mr Phillips said:

> The heart of the mission given by Parliament to the Equality and Human Rights Commission is to ensure that, even in the worst of time, our destiny is not limited by our origins. That our life chances are not merely the sum of our parents' backgrounds and the racial or gender category into which we are born. That our success or failure does not become the hostage of age, religion, belief or disability. That our ambitions are not frustrated by the whims of bureaucratic or oppressive authority...[1]

Such a statement makes little sense to me (see below, p. 99*ff*): but Mr Phillips seems to be at home in this sub-messianic vein. On 17 June 2008 he said:

> Whatever the political weather, when governments change and pressure groups wilt... one day this Commission, and I hope it doesn't have to happen on my watch, could be the last best hope of those who really believe that we should be a more equal society; of those who think that human rights and civil liberties are

> sacrosanct; of those who believe that there should always be a voice for the poor and dispossessed… the public want us to be the conscience of the nation… to be the ones who hold our society to the hope, the promise of being better than it is today… We are dealing with something that, in terms of urgency and scale, is on a par with climate change if not more significant.[2]

On 23 February 2009, in what seems to be a more modest and focused statement of mission, he told Decca Aitkenhead of the G2 Interview that:

> The task is not to shout for black people or women, but to break the grip of white men who went to public school. And that's why I'm here.[3]

In a variant of this, in November 2010 Yasmin Alibhai-Brown, a member of the Parekh Commission, journalist and midwife-mother to British Muslims for a Secular Democracy: a 'moderate' organisation dedicated to 'co-existence and harmony', said:

> I look around every single institution in Britain and I see a white man's world. I'm not saying people in power in these institutions are sitting around being racist, but they are sitting around making decisions that continue to create a highly discriminatory and unrepresentative world.[4]

Mrs Alibhai-Brown's mother was cut from a different cloth, telling her daughter that she:

> should show some respect for the old citizens of Britain for sharing their small island with them, and that they [had given her] a pension, and me, my independence. 'They didn't look at my face and refuse me that did they? I know you [addressing her daughter] are fighting for equality but life is not perfect.'[5]

At first reading, the authors of the EHRC Report would appear to have paid more (but not much) attention to the Mrs Alibhai-Brown's mother than to the more acerbic daughter. In Chapter 14, 'Power and Voice', and in what seems to be a commendation, it describes Britain as having 'many forms of democracy [which] exist side by side'. We soon move, though, away from the mother and towards the daughter, the Report going on to show its ignorance of (or indifference to?) one 'form' of our democracy, that propounded by Edmund Burke in his address to the electors of Bristol. Burke said very clearly that elected representatives must be more concerned with national than mere sectional interests. He would not have approved of the Report's definition and commendation of our 'representative democracy' as a system which 'allows adults to vote for people who reflect their interests in local authorities and national Parliaments'.[6] In offering and saluting this version of 'democracy' the authors of the EHRC Report demonstrate that they see it as nothing more than a vehicle for the expression of sectional interests. Here, as elsewhere, they busy themselves with sawing off the very log on which they so comfortably sit: a rabble of small boys in playground would have more chance of social harmony and stability than a crowd of lonely self-promoting minorities headed by their equally self-promoting and blinkered representatives.

The EHRC Report evidently approves of its page 576 definition of 'representative democracy'—but this is not enough. In one of the Report's frequent '*howevers*', it moves even further away from the good sense of the mother and gets alongside both the daughter (Yasmin) and Mr Trevor Phillips, saying that: 'Professionals are more likely to vote, to hold office and more likely to feel that they can influence local decisions than people from lower occupational groups'[7] and that 'MPs are disproportionately from higher socio-economic groups'.[8] We seem to be back with the prime enemy, white men who went to public school, thus insufficiently 'representative'!

Albeit, we move on with Mr Phillips. In commenting on an opinion poll taken after the election of Barack Obama, Mr Phillips said that while he had 'faith in the basic decency of the British people... we can't be complacent', and he referred to 'emerging religious divisions' (Bombs and murders? How bland a comment!) and to the need to 'work harder to keep up with an Obama generation so positive about the future and the diversity of Britain'.[9]

Why should President Obama be the standard? Perhaps because the scions of Parekh + Macpherson + Phillips + EHRC see in him, the first black President of the USA, the embodiment of their own activities over several decades of multiculturalism? Or perhaps because the President's career, while obviously rising to greater heights (and to serious responsibilities) is quite close in shape to the careers of Mr Phillips and others who belong, to adapt the usage of Indian social commentators, to the 'creamy layer' of the discriminated-against world? (See below p. 62*ff.*) And not just Mr Phillips: amongst those 'working harder' to keep the British up to the mark are the 14 Commissioners under whose guidance the 750 page Report was produced. They are now part of the 'Establishment', having risen to this position by, of, through, and alongside their hard-work and championship of minority and ethnic rights. Britain's experiment with multiculturalism is of short duration compared with India's, from which we get the phrase 'creamy layer' and from which we can probably learn some lessons.

8

The EHRC—a Creamy Layer?

While we have had the EHRC for but two years, India has for some decades had a National Commission for Backward Classes, which, through a complex system of quotas, tries to promote the educational and occupational rights of what it rather quaintly calls the 'backward classes', the 'very backward classes' and 'other backward classes'. It does this in part by seeking to limit the advantages of the 'forward classes'.[1] At both central and lower or state levels, India's politicians have long been used to various types of coalition governments (again like Great Britain now), where votes and electoral success are to some extent determined by being 'sensitive' to the quotas. One of the consequences of the Indian policy has been the creation of what are whimsically 'creamy layers', which refers to two groups: one, those more enterprising or lucky members of a 'backward class' who through being 'discriminated for' by a government agency, somehow get a grip on a reasonably well-paid 'quota' job; and two, those publicly-paid civil servants whose job it is to administer the quota. There is a degree of overlap between these two: who better, after all, to both exemplify and at the same time moderate the effects of institutional racism than the victim? The Indian system has another interesting feature: it has a degree of wisdom about 'corruption'. India is a federal state: and now and then rather painfully spawns new ethnic-area states whose leaders welcome the transfer of federal funds as both means and inducement to them to 'resist centrifugal tendencies'—a euphemism for irredentist armed mobilisations. Sometimes, the leaders of one-time irredentist movements become 'respectable', and as part of their settlement with the federal authorities in Delhi, they become the channels for the receipt and disbursement of federal funds. As a kind of insurance policy, the Indian government also maintains about a million para-military troops, stationed in areas prone to irredentism and violence—rather like the British Raj once did.

Britain has its creamy layers. One of the predecessors of the EHRC was the Commission for Racial Equality (Chair Trevor Phillips), which together with the Home Office and other government departments produced a series of consultation documents and policies concerned with 'perception targets' (quotas by any other name), aiming at building a 'more representative' public sector work force. Quotas are very much part of the 'equality' agenda. Given this, and given the remarks about white men made by Messrs Phillips and Alibhai-Brown, perhaps we should consider in this chapter the current EHRC as part of the 'creamy layer' of British quota politics. (Creamy Layers come in many forms, see below, but few perhaps as droll in provenance as Mrs Yasmin Alibhai-Brown's own British Muslims for a Secular Democracy, part-funded by the City Parochial Foundation, which in turn lives off an accumulation of 1,400 charitable gifts and bequests, many made centuries ago by white Christians males to their parishes for the relief of the poor of those parishes.)

From *FO1419*, a document kindly sent to me by one of 445 employees of the EHRC, and from other sources, we learn that there are 14 Commissioners. Of the 14 Commissioners, seven would appear to have had, or have, involvement with the Labour Party and Trade Unions, one with the Liberals. Four would appear to be peers of one kind or another, and eight have either the CBE or the OBE. Ten are female. Other qualifications, accomplishments and positions present us with a picture of an 'unequal' or 'disproportionate' number of those 'higher socio-economic groups' of which the EHRC Report is so critical.[2] There are 445 full-time equivalent employees. The Commissioners are paid for approved duties at the rate of £500 per day, with a maximum number of days permitted ranging from 3.5 days per week for Mr Phillips as Chair, down to 20-30 days per year for the other Commissioners. Reimbursement is available for travelling expenses, subsistence and hotels. The congestion charge is payable if incurred unavoidably on official business. Taxi fares are payable, on production of a receipt, when for example, heavy luggage has to be carried between railway stations. The EHRC has a travel booking service. Reasonable childcare costs are claimable. There is an allowance of 40p a mile for the first 10,000 miles of car use, of 20p a mile for pedal bicycle use; and a variety of accommodation expenses, including one of £25 if staying overnight with a friend. The EHRC has entered into a special arrangement with HMRC to handle the tax consequences of these various forms of income and benefit. The Chair, Mr Phillips, has a car and driver, which is available also for the Deputy Chair and senior staff.[3]

The denizens of Creamy Layers, being part-time, are not always too well advised about money matters, though they ran a budget of £53 million, 2010/11. In 2009 the National Audit Office felt obliged to report to the House of Commons Committee of Public Accounts[4] on what appeared to be irregular accounting practices at the newly-created EHRC. The NAO reported that:

> The EHRC incurred costs of £629,276 in respect of the severance costs of three individuals, but, on returning to the Commission, these staff received between them consultancy fees of £323,708. The Treasury had not authorised in advance the payments to re-engage these staff, and refused to do so retrospectively because it did not consider the payments represented value for money. In particular, the Treasury expressed concern about the level of the salaries paid to the re-engaged staff and raised the possibility that the re-engaged staff should have repaid their severance payments.[5]

The House of Commons Committee shared these concerns—and had others:

> Serious errors were made in setting up the Commission... The Commission now accepts that it was not ready for business... and that its set-up process, which cost £39 million, was flawed and inefficient. The Commission's Chairman recognised his personal share of responsibility and told us that the Board did not exercise the level of scrutiny it might have done, despite early warning signs being clearly visible.[6]

At the time of writing, the budget of the Commission, now firmly under the Government

Equalities Office, faces some heavy cuts. However, Creamy Layers usually survive and indeed come out on top—if not as institutions, at least as honorific elevation for their denizens.

Section Three

9

A Thin Blue Line—the British Police and Some New British Criminals

When, many years ago, I was involved at a local level with 'race relations' it always surprised me how frequently the representatives of various minority groups would refer to their 'good relationships' with the police. As a local councillor, and a long-time resident of the toughest part of Newcastle, the police never seemed to me to be 'a problem' in the sense of being a threat—far from it: life would have been, and indeed still is, impossible without their minatory presence. I just took them for granted. In the 1950s I would have been among those who conformed to Geoffrey Gorer's finding that the majority of British people have 'an enthusiastic appreciation of the English police'.[1] Gorer, in a manner seemingly light years away from the Era of Macpherson, asserts that: 'To a great extent, the police represent an ideal mode of behaviour and character', especially for young people under 18, where 82 per cent have a positive view of the police.[2] He quotes a 22-year-old unmarried working-class girl from Hendon: 'I think the police do a wonderful job, and would never think of criticising them. Although I have no reason at all for fearing them, I always regard them with respect and a certain amount of awe.'[3] That was and is my view.

The police and the criminal justice system would appear not to have the same kind of relationship with ethnic minorities. At the time of writing, there is considerable press coverage of the conviction of a number of Pakistani men for 'grooming' and raping young white girls for sexual purposes and for leading or forcing them into prostitution. As already mentioned, on BBC Radio Four 8 January 2011 former Home Secretary Jack Straw, MP for Blackburn, commented that there were clearly young Pakistani men 'fizzing and popping with testosterone' (a peculiarly Pakistani problem?), regarding white girls as 'easy targets and easy meat', while 'Pakistani-heritage girls were off-limits'. On the same programme a police spokesman said that the police would not be deterred by possible accusations of 'racism' when and where there was very obviously a 'disproportionate prevalence' of certain kinds of behaviour amongst some groups of young men with whom the police felt that they should and would 'engage'. An ex-policemen ('name and address supplied') told the *Sunday Times* how 'heartened' he was to see the issue of 'young white girls [being] groomed for sex by Pakistani males finally being confronted' and how 'the police service seems to have become paranoid about the race issue'.[4]

The EHRC Report spends large parts of two chapters on the relationship between ethnic minorities and the British police and the criminal justice system. So, for example, we have figures on various types of crime, on attitudes to the service provided by the police and on stop and search and on the profile of ethnic minorities in prison. We know (see p. 33 above) that the EHRC intervened to change police regulations about 'stop and search'. In the section of the Report called 'What we know about homicide', we are told that of 2,200 homicides recorded in England and Wales 2006/09, and where the ethnic identity of the victim is known, 516 were from an ethnic minority and of these over half were black.[5] Nothing is said about the ethnic identity of the killers, many of whom are also black.

Between pages 108 and 117 we have figures for deaths in institutions, including deaths in police custody. The bar chart is rather difficult to read, and the data are problematic, but the Report quotes a Parliamentary Committee for Human Rights which states that between 1998 and 2003, 18 per cent of those who died in police custody were from ethnic minorities. It is tempting to point out that when ethnic minorities *as victim* are being statistically described, the presentation stops there, free of complaint of 'racialising' the figures. When statistics on ethnic minorities *as offenders* make an appearance, then they are either dismissed as 'racialising' or lavered with great soap-suds of sociology, the deviant behaviour being 'explained' by—'*a high proportion of young people'* or '*poverty'* or '*unemployment'* or '*identity problems'* or, as we have seen, *testosterone*...

Chapters 7 (Legal Security) and 8 (Physical Security), are amongst the longest in the Report. Chapter 7 starts with the statement that 'the majority of people believe that accused people will be treated fairly by the criminal justice system'. This is followed immediately by yet another of the Report's *howevers*, this one stating that ethnic minorities are less likely to think that complaints against the police will be taken seriously and that they are more likely to fear police harassment. On page 137, *however*—if I too may be permitted a *however*—we learn that 'more people from ethnic minority backgrounds were confident that the CJS as a whole was fair: 68 per cent, compared with 57 per cent of white people'. *However* (again!), we are told that 'an in-depth study of young ethnic minority people's attitudes suggested that young black people remain wary of being perceived as criminals by the police'. 'In-depth' means a study of 47 young black men. This flow of *howevers* has, of course, the effect of shifting the emphasis away from the main point: 'the majority of people believe that accused people will be treated fairly by the criminal justice system' and 'more people from ethnic minority backgrounds were confident that the CJS as a whole was fair: 68 per cent, compared with 57 per cent of white people'. Even if 47 young black men were a fully representative sample, why is that *in any* sense the logical follow-up to the much more interesting finding that ethnic minorities are more at ease with the police than are we whites? Why dodge what the EHRC Report's own figures show?

This chapter has a figure for domestic violence against (mostly) women.[6] There were 1,641,000 victims in 2007/08. The number of women actually *killed* by 'a partner or ex-partner' rose above 100 for the first time in four years. On page 153, Box 7.2.2 comments on '"Honour" crimes, forced marriage, trafficking and female genital mutilation'. Beyond saying that the figures for these things which are available are 'the tip of the iceberg', little is said, in the Box, about how ethnic minorities figure in such practices. On page 155, however, we are told that:

> some women from ethnic minorities who have experienced rape or domestic violence face barriers to accessing criminal justice agencies. Partly, these reflect a lack of cultural sensitivity within the CJS. Black and

> ethnic minority people experiencing domestic abuse, as a result, have been found to be less likely than White people to access statutory services. Many women from ethnic minority backgrounds fear reporting domestic violence because of the ramifications for and within their communities.

Does 'ramifications' mean that they fear they might be killed? This curious travel through this grim topic of violence continues in Chapter 8, 'Physical Security'. On page 220 we get: 'There are no significant differences between ethnic groups in relation to violence—partly (*sic*) because of the small numbers involved'. The ubiquitous 'however' then takes us to a comment that *mixed*-race (my emphasis) people have a higher (four per cent) rate of violence 'partly because they are disproportionately young': while 'violence seems to be less common among other ethnic minority groups (two per cent) than it is among white people'.

On 'Domestic violence' we are told that: 'Data from the British Crime Survey suggest that there are no significant differences between ethnic and religious minority groups in relation to domestic violence, however [*again!*] they face particular vulnerabilities'.[7] We are then referred to Box 8.1.4, where the data seem to relate primarily to refugees, migrants, gypsies and travellers, i.e. a minority of a minority, with quite specific problems. The authors seem to have forgotten an earlier Box 8.1.1,[8] which deals with '"Honour" killings, female genital mutilation, forced marriages and trafficking', for which 'there is (*sic*) no national survey data, given the dangers of disclosure to those who are victims'.

I find it hard to believe that data about such activities, with the exception perhaps of 'trafficking', would have been even collected in, say, the Dixon of Dock Green era of 1950s, when they would have been unknown. 'Honour' killings (what a description for this despicable dreadful activity), female genital mutilation, forced marriages—surely, a feature of multi-ethnic Britain, imported along with their practitioners? Indeed, the Report itself, having bemoaned the lack of 'national survey data', tells us on the same page, and quoting from an article by Walby *et al.*, that there were in England alone about 5,000 to 8,000 cases of actual or threatened forced marriages, *that the majority (97 per cent) were within the Asian community, with forced marriage being a particularly (72 per cent) Pakistani practice* (my emphases)—significant differences, surely? We end with an odd interpolation: 'There is growing evidence of a rise in forced/sham marriages among LGB [lesbian, gay and bisexual] people'.[9] Neither figures nor percentages are given for this datum, so oddly introduced.

Neither the EHRC nor this particular Report has a monopoly of these tactics of deliberate or protective obfuscation (but by their example they condone them). In 2009 I attended a seminar on forced marriage organised by the Government Office for the North East and addressed by, amongst others, Jasminder Sanghera, the redoubtable Director of Karma Nirvana and by a speaker from the Forced Marriage Unit of the Home Office.[10] The speaker put up a slide with some statistics on the national or ethnic bases of forced marriage, as the Home Office had them. The figures showed that Pakistanis accounted for 65 per cent,

Bangladeshis for 15-20 per cent, and Indians (Sikhs, Hindus, Muslims) eight per cent. It would, he volunteered, be a mistake to see this as a Muslim issue, as there were, for example, cases in Mauritius and Ireland, and 'what about Romeo and Juliet?': 'It is not', he said, 'just a Muslim issue and no major religion condones it, and religion is rarely involved in forced marriage, it's often land or money or family links…'

All this while the slide was on the screen showing that 80-85 per cent of cases, on his own figures, involved, demonstrably, Muslims! If he had put on the screen a figure showing that 80-85 per cent of Grand National winners had three legs then I would forthwith have gone out and bet my house on a three-legged horse. There seems no way of penetrating official, amiable, helpful, stupid occlusive decencies. As I write, and as I have already mentioned, the BBC and the *Guardian* are part of the process of casting a veil of look-away prudery over the sentencing of a group of Pakistani men for rape and sexual exploitation of young white girls, an event worth revisiting. Even *The Times*, which 'broke' the story, had two articles asserting in effect that 'we're to blame' for these crimes.[11] Why is stupidity on such matters a virtue? No one disputes the fact that many/most sexual offenders are white—most British people are white! Most people who travel on a bus are white. This does not mean that the Asian-Pakistani offenders are *not* offenders; and if there are specific 'sociologies' around their depredations, and if these sociologies show higher rates per thousand or per hundred thousand, i.e. a disproportionate offence, then these offences need to be identified and dealt with, whether they are to do with religion, culture or the fizzing and popping of testosterone. In the meantime, none of these reasons are excuses and men who do these things must be punished.

The issue of 'ordinary' (non-terrorist) Muslim crime is a very serious one, which I have dealt with in an earlier book, *In Search of the Moderate Muslim*.[12] Muslim men represent a radically disproportionate number of prisoners, convicted of 'ordinary' crimes, there being about 9,000 to 10,000 in prison at any one time; there is a very high rate of recidivism.[13] Sikh and Hindu prisoners are counted in hundreds. Muslim writers such as Yahya Birt attest to this problem.[14] This pool of Muslim prisoners and ex-prisoners will constitute the 'sea' within which some very much nastier creatures live and lurk; and they must give their 'communities', the police, the security services and us a very real problem. I make further comment on this, below.

Macpherson dealt the police a grievous blow—they are, said the judge, irrefutably (because 'institutionally'), a racist organisation, serving a racist society. Strange, then, that the police seem to have, if the EHRC Report and its sources are correct, the support and confidence of the majority of the members of ethnic minorities, the very people who are, or should be, the recipients of their 'institutional racism'. As already quoted, in Chapter 7 we are told that 'the majority of people believe that accused people will be treated fairly by the criminal justice system'.[15] We are not given the figures: and this is followed immediately by another of the Report's *howevers*, this one stating that ethnic minorities are less likely to think that complaints against the police will be taken seriously and that they are more likely to fear police harassment—again, no figures: 'less likely', of course, could still be a majority!

The EHRC Report sometimes uses the British Crime Survey, as I did when writing *In Search of the Moderate Muslim* (see p. 78*ff*). It would appear that our institutionally racist police are quite highly thought of by what the British Crime Survey calls 'self-defined Asians'. Over the years 2001 to 2007 a high percentage of self-defined Asians (of between the mid- to high 70s in percentage terms) reported that they 'had confidence in the way the CJS handled crime suspects'. Whites had the same level of confidence, while blacks came in at the mid-60 per cent. For 2006-7, that is *after* the London bombings, 76 per cent of self-defined Asians and 79 per cent of self-defined whites had confidence in the CJS, and 76 per cent of self-defined Asians felt that the CJS 'respected the rights of suspects'. For that same year, 53 per cent of self-defined Asians felt that the CJS 'met the need of crime victims', as compared with 31 per cent of self-defined whites. From a 2001 Home Office Report we get the figure of 63 per cent of Pakistanis and Bangladeshis who expressed satisfaction on making contact with the police, as opposed to 67 per cent of black people, 62 per cent of Indians and 72 per cent of whites.[16] Generally, Asians (like the rest of us) have high levels of satisfaction with the police.

In 1955 Geoffrey Gorer published his findings on the relationship between the British police and the British public. Gorer reported that the majority of British people (73 per cent of men, 74 per cent of women) had positive views of the police.[17] This varied from region to region (highest in the North West at 78 per cent and lowest in the North East and North at 69 per cent) and by class (79 per cent for the upper middle class, 65 per cent for the lower working classes). He reported that young people under the age of 18 were, at 82 per cent, particularly positive about the police. Gorer was, of course, writing before surveys recognised or disaggregated ethnic minorities: Britain was white.

There is some scepticism, now, about surveys of the public attitude to the police—see the blog of 'Inspector Gadget', and his book *Perverting the Course of Justice; the hilarious and shocking inside story of British policing*.[18] Yet, give or take a few percentage points, there is not much difference between Gorer's figures (The Dixon of Dock Green Era?) and those reported by the BCS and the EHRC Report—though Gorer does without the *howevers*. The British police would appear to have maintained a high degree of public approbation over a period (1950-2010) of extraordinary social change, of rapidly rising crime (with or without its association with immigration), of the arrival of ethnic minorities with very different values, of sexual liberation and, in general, of a society wallowing in the visible sleaze and squalor of affluence. It is difficult to 'locate' Macpherson in all of this, except perhaps to suggest that his major accomplishment has been to wreck police morale, on which Gorer reported so favourably. As my good and sorely missed friend Norman Dennis wrote in a book which should be read by all responsible citizens:

> The Macpherson report has had a detrimental effect on policing and crime, particularly in London. Police morale

> has been undermined. Certain procedures which impact disproportionately on ethnic groups, like stop and search, have been scaled down. The crime rate has risen. Nevertheless, the Macpherson report has been received with almost uncritical approval by pundits, politicians and academics. It is still routinely described as having 'proved' that the police and British society are racist.[19]

Macpherson was much praised in his time. Perhaps the time has now come to bury him and his sundry offspring. Perhaps I am naïve: so lest such a statement elicit an accusation of 'golden ageism', and shouts of 'Dixon of Dock Green', perhaps I can repeat what I wrote above. *When you take the reported data on public attitudes to and experience of the police, then there is not much difference between Gorer's data from the middle of the twentieth century and the British Crime Survey data for the first decade of the twenty-first century. From these data, flawed certainly, but the best we have, we see that the public's view of the police is much closer to Gorer than to Macpherson; and this is as or more true of ethnic minorities living in Britain than it is of the white indigenous population.*

This is really rather remarkable, given that the police now face criminal elements with which Dixon of Dock Green was not familiar. Macpherson reported against the back-drop of the problematic relations between the police and black men: indeed, the Metropolitan Police has separate units to deal specifically with 'black' crime. Less publicly visible, other than 'terrorism', is the high level of 'ordinary' criminality amongst Muslims resident in Britain, described in the Report as making up 10-12 per cent of the prison population.[20] The only comment made by the authors of the Report on this extraordinary figure is to draw attention to the treatment of Muslims *while in prison*—Muslims have provision for their religious needs (while other minority religions experience a 'less consistent' provision); Muslim male prisoners are more likely to be on the basic 'no privileges' regime; and that they are more likely to feel unsafe and to complain of maltreatment by the staff than do non-Muslims. No comment at all is made on the very low proportions of prisoners who are Hindu, Sikh or Jewish—or how or what they feel. Christians get no mention.

On 24 July 2005, a uniformed member of the Association of Chief Police Officers (ACPO) addressed a meeting at the Regent's Park Islamic Centre. This was just after the time of the London bombs. The Chief Constable introduced himself with *'salaam alekum'*, told the gathering of Muslims that Islam was a 'great religion' which the police did not understand; he said that the recent bombs were a great shock; and that he, the reputed ACPO expert, did not in fact know much about the Muslim community as *'we police around your communities, but not in them'*.[21] The police, he said, needed the community to help them, and the police in turn pledged themselves to protect Muslims in these difficult times, that they would deal with Islamophobia and hate crime, *inshallah* (applause). Later, Tariq Ramadan, a Muslim intellectual and academic, berated the audience for not being fully cognizant of the society in which they lived, i.e. Great Britain.[22] From these two opinions, we get a picture of a somewhat troubled relationship between the police and Muslims and between the majority society and Muslims.

I have dealt more fully with the matter of the Muslim crime wave in an earlier book,[23] and here perhaps need do no more than to repeat the words of Yahya Birt, a Muslim convert (or revert, as Muslims say) who says that:

> The surge in Muslim crime is not being discussed openly within the community… probably out of a sense of shame. But in reality we should feel ashamed because we are not facing these problems openly and discussing them.[24]

The Security Services currently keep watch on about 2,000 would-be terrorists or terrorist cells. This issue is cheerfully ignored by the Report. If 1,000 of these terrorists or cells are Muslim, and adding to it at least a few of the hundreds of Muslim prisoners coming in and out of prison in any one year, then do we not have the intra- and inter-communal makings of a seriously 'unfair' policing problem? Marie Macey certainly thinks so: she refers to 'criminal and neo-criminal behaviour having a massive negative impact' on her city of Bradford, 'creating a negative image of the city that not only discourages inward investment and job creation [but is also] causing established business to relocate'.[25] In the strange bland world of the EHRC, none of this seems to matter. The police have always to be seen dressed in the garb of institutional racism.

10

The Unfair World in Which We Live

In 1919, 44 nation states signed the Covenant of the League of Nations. In 1945, 50 nation states set up the United Nations. By 1956 the UN had 80 members. There are now about 192 nation states, created recently at the rate of about two a year—and counting: 204 countries competed at the 2008 Summer Olympics. The histories of these nation states are different in many ways. Many of them have travelled, more or less successfully, a political path from tribe to empire and then out the other side, as it were, as nation. Others, ancient nations temporarily subdued, just reappeared. After centuries of these varied processes, it would seem that the 'the nation state' is the preferred option: tribes (which in some places are still problematically alive within the bosom of the new nation state) were essentially military units, with war being the main male business: and there has never been a peaceful empire. Nations states are not perfect, but they seem to be the way the world now wishes to live.

We hear a lot—especially from the multiculturalists—about globalisation. Yet figures for 2003/5 show that 97 per cent of the world's population will breed and die where it was born: less than three per cent are international migrants.[1] The 97 per cent are the unlucky ones. The migrants and their progeny are the smart and lucky ones. I in no way underestimate what it costs to emigrate or to try to emigrate and what it is to live in a minority community in an alien land.

The word 'nation' comes from the Latin *nasci* or *natus,* to be born, indicating membership by birth, carrying with it amongst other things the connotation of 'no choice'. When the word 'race' is brought in, then we have Latin *radix,* a root, or Greek *rhiza,* a root or shoot. Both words indicate something fixed, and fixed to a particular place. It is thus something indeed over which—for better or for worse!—most of us have little choice. I did not choose to be born British: but my failure to pass the Official Citizenship Test for Life in the United Kingdom, given to me by my (Slovakian) daughter-in-law, in no way diminishes the fixity of my birth, my nationality, my Britishness. Foreigners have to pass this exam. I do not. I do not even have to sit it. I am stuck with the limitations of my birth. I consider myself lucky to have had my life so restricted.

For all these nation states, in all their varied pedigrees, we now have, for the first time ever in the history of the world, genuinely sound data. We are not dependent on the stories of Marco Polo or Ibn Khaldun or Alberuni for knowledge of the world. We know, more rather than less, what life is like in all or most of these 200 or so nation states: we can compare them and ask: where would you prefer to live, if you had the choice? Where is there a democratic government, and where does the government complement rather than crush its people? Where is there less corruption? Where are the police, armed and aggressive, an internal oppressive force and where are the police, unarmed as a matter of routine, subject to the law? Where will your wife deliver her children in some degree of safety, and where will her children survive and flourish? Where will the fruits of your work be cumulative *and inheritable,* and not subject to depredations, theft, flood and civil war? Which society is fairer—not perfect, but fairer? Where would you prefer to live?

When we consider those ethnic minorities who have, in very large numbers since the 1960s, chosen to live here, then we can compare the places they or their fathers and forefathers left with the place they chose to come to—the place, Great Britain, indeed, in which their descendants appear to want to live. Where the data permit (as not all nation states are so bureaucratically or rationally organised as to generate systematic data) I will compare Great Britain with India, Pakistan and Bangladesh. Occasionally, I will refer to other states, primarily from Africa, a continent which seems to produce many an asylum seeker. The data I provide are available on the web.[2] Certainly, the data and their sources have problems: but add them all together for an answer to the questions immediately above.

Freedom House provides a Map of Freedom in the World in which countries are ranked on a scale of 1-7, 1 being the highest, for 'Political Rights' and 'Civil Liberties', and then an overall 'Status'. Thus the United Kingdom scores a 1 for Political Rights, a 1 for Civil Liberties and an overall status-assessment as 'Free'. India is also classified as 'Free', scoring a 2* for 'Political Rights' and a 2* for 'Civil Liberties', the * indicating the concern for the Kashmir issue. Pakistan is classified as 'Partly Free', and gets a 4 for Political Rights and a 5 for Civil Liberties. Bangladesh is classified as 'Partly Free' and gets a 3 for Political Rights and a 4 for Civil Liberties.

Let us dismiss Freedom House as a tool of the United States, as most of its funding comes from the US government.

The Global Peace Index, published by the Institute of Peace and Economic Studies, ranks 149 countries on the basis of an 'absence of violence': the higher the number, the more violence and turmoil within that nation state. On this scale, the UK scores 31, India 128, Pakistan 145 and Bangladesh 147. The Index compilers note that an improvement of 10 points increases per capita income by $3,100: good order and tranquillity are good for business. India in 2007 was ranked 109 and 122 in 2009.[3]

The Capital Punishment Index, available on MSN Encarta, provides details on how many countries have capital punishment, how many countries have it but use it relatively infrequently, and how many use it often. As an aside, China provides the world with a high proportion of its capital punishment cases. The UK has none and has no legal facility for capital punishment. Bangladesh had its last executions in 2010; Pakistan in 2008; India in 2004. The judicial system of all three countries, clearly, retains capital punishment.

Transparency International provides data on corruption.[4] Of the 170 countries listed, the UK scores 20, India 87, Pakistan 143, Bangladesh 134. For five years after 2005, Bangladesh had the dubious distinction of being classified as the world's most corrupt country. The compilers of this Index state that globally corruption/bribery costs, at a conservative estimate, one trillion US dollars; that in Africa a bribery score of $148 billion adds 20 per cent to the costs of goods and services; and that even small reductions in corruption result in substantial increases in per capita incomes and reductions in infant mortality.

The Press Freedom Index, published by Reporters without Borders, has an Index covering 178 countries. In the 2010 Index, the UK is in at 19, having improved its position: both India (122) and Bangladesh (126) are regarded as getting worse, while Pakistan (151) is improving but has a long, long way to go.[5]

The World Economic Forum produces the Global Competitiveness Index, ranking 131 countries on how effectively they use available resources: 'the set of institutions, policies and factors that determine the level of productivity of a country'. Bangladesh, India and Pakistan are all classified in Stage One of Development, roughly measured as a per capita income of less that $2,000, while the UK is in Stage 3, with a per capita income of more than $17,000. The WEF describes itself as 'Committed to improving the state of the world'.[6]

The Legatum Prosperity Index 2010 ranks 110 countries in terms of their economy, their capacity for entrepreneurship and opportunity, governance, education, health, safety and security, personal freedom and social capital: the UK is ranked 18, India 88, Bangladesh 96, Pakistan 109 (just above Zimbabwe). Some interesting detail is made available: thus, for 2009, only 82 per cent of Bangladeshis feel possessed of 'personal safety'.

The UN's Human Development Index is perhaps the most comprehensive cover of the state of the world, describing itself as measuring 'the real wealth of nations: pathways to human development'. In its

2010 report it provides data for 169 countries. The HDI does for the world what the EHRC said it did for Britain. 'Human development' covers all or most of the criteria of well being—life expectancy, literacy, education, food, etc. It was developed by two economists, Mahbub ul Haq, a Pakistani, and Amartya Sen, an Indian. Here the United Kingdom at 26 is in the 'Very High' category for human development (the top 10 are all European or European-origin countries): India at 119, and Pakistan at 125, are in the 'Medium' category, while Bangladesh at 129 is in the Low category.

There can be no doubt from such a range of data that Britain is Best—or Better than India, Pakistan, Bangladesh: it would be foolish to migrate from here to, say, Pakistan in the expectation that life-chances for you or your children would be fairer there. To say this, of course, is to invite the accusation not only of triumphalism but also the retort that Britain is Best at the expense of the rest. The retort is by now wearing thin: and is rarely heard from countries such as China, which simply takes the evidence of its earlier humiliations by 'the West' as proof of its success in overcoming them. In India, too, we now hear the same song: *Jai Hind*!

As for the charge of 'triumphalism' it is surely not necessary to say that things change, and that the global rankings of today will not be those of the next decades: change and decay in all around we see. We in Britain are very vulnerable to dropping down these various tables: the future is not bright for my grandchildren. At the moment, though, our performance seems *FAIR*.

Far from this parade of global data leading necessarily to triumphalism (white, English, British, European or otherwise) does it not more logically lead to a deep sense of *gratitude*—a finer mode of participation in our national story than this endless call for rights and their self-pitying slogans of 'unfairness'? An insistence on the transcendent virtue of gratitude, not rights, is not something to be imposed solely upon immigrants or their descendants. As much as any immigrant, or descendant of immigrant, I too am the heir to the hard work, good sense and good luck of my ancestors—*my* ancestors, note. In the city in which I live, the central monument—known simply as the Monument—commemorates the passing of the Great Reform Bill of 1832 (a document which is apparently over 60 yards long!). On the front of the Monument is to be found the customary rather florid Victorian eulogy of Prime Minister Earl Grey (who took 38 years to get his measure through Parliament!). As interesting as the eulogy on the front are the words to be found on the reverse of the Monument, in which in 1932 the people of the United Kingdom express their gratitude to the author of the Great Reform Bill '*for a century of civil peace*'. No other country in the world could make such a claim. Further, this 'century of civil peace', when extraordinary social and economic changes took place, itself depended on earlier progress in nation building. Overcoming civil war and foreign war, and dynastic and constitutional struggle, the British economy grew steadily: since 1750 there has been a rate of increase of productivity per head per annum of between 1.5 per cent to 2 per cent, giving a seven-fold increase over a century, or a 65 per cent increase every generation of 25 years or so.[7] None of this was easy: and it was certainly easier (less fair?) for some than others.

As it happens, I am Welsh. My paternal great-grandfather, son of an agricultural labourer in South West Wales, migrated from the land and went, age 6, with his father (my great-great grandfather), down the pits newly opening in the Rhondda—part of the advantage being that the work was not seasonal! Another advantage was that the agricultural skills with horses of my great-great grandfather were transferable to the pits, which too had horses (somewhat smaller ones). My grandfather went to work in the mines aged 12—a 100 per cent improvement over *his* father!—and in the winter, going to work before first light and returning after sundown, saw the sun only on Sunday. Later, at age 30 or so, being too ill to continue down the mine, he earned a living with a horse and cart selling soap, detergents, paraffin and other household equipment in the valleys of South Wales. To do this he would leave before first light, my grandmother getting up with him to make up his 'box'. He had had to leave school early (i.e. age 12) because his parents needed his wages to pay the costs of educating his siblings: he was a literate man, a poet, but an unfair world did not pay poets. My own father was the prototypical Welsh grammar school boy. Fluent in both English and Welsh, he went to the relatively new Aberystwyth College or University. This college was in large measure built or maintained by half-crowns donated by ordinary working people—miners, quarrymen and agricultural labourers. On *Sul y Brifysgol* ('University Sunday') the hundreds of chapels in Wales, themselves communal or congregational creations, collected money for the college at Aberystwyth.[8] From many a chapel pulpit and from many a Sunday School, a poor and rough people derived a moral life-compass which made them the authors of their own lives. The miners' libraries, philosophical societies, choirs, temperance societies and (even!) their rugby teams were not provided for them by some early version of the EHRC: they were developed by themselves, out of the very hardness of the lives they led; and developed so as to provide themselves and (more importantly) their children with a means of coping with a life of a rigour and toughness few of us now experience.

My maternal grandfather went, as a boy, to sea to escape the cruelty of his alcoholic father (who died in the insane section of the local workhouse). At sea, he earned his Master's ticket, and eventually owned and operated several small ships, trading across the Irish Sea and in and out of the Dee and the Mersey. His eldest son was killed when his ship, taking shelter in the Mersey to avoid German bombs, was run down and sunk by a Royal Navy warship. Their hard work, though, was inheritable through the property they laboured to buy and through the education they obtained for their children.

I am the heir to all of this. I have no rights to this inheritance. How can I have a right to what I did not make? I owe. I owe a debt of gratitude to it and to my ancestors, kin and otherwise, who made it all possible. I am a guest in it, a guest of long-standing, but a guest no less. The appeal of a language of 'rights' is neutralised by the language of gratitude, of obligation, of a real and routine awareness that I walk upon a stage I have not built. This 'stage' is made up of a massive array of collective goods—power lines and clean water, schools and hospitals, flat footpaths, kerbed roads, unarmed and honest police, sewers, a common language, national parks and local libraries—wealth, indeed, not available to many or most of the people still living in the various countries-of-origin covered or mentioned above. We, here, are all well off. I no doubt exaggerate: but not as much as the preacher at a black Caribbean church in Birmingham who, seeking to explain the disproportionate number of black men in prison, and their poor performance in school, refuted the 'pull yourself up by your bootstrap' injunction by saying that it was no use to those who had no boots.[9] Pulpits engender exaggeration, no doubt, as does exposure to the media. Perhaps black women wear the boots in black Caribbean households. On the evidence of the EHRC Report, and much other data, black women outperform their men in many ways—except crime.

People who have come here, to the land my ancestors made (and indeed a land from which many of my ancestors emigrated), have access to a good and valuable resource. There can surely be no doubt whatsoever that the incomes of Pakistanis, Bangladeshis and Indians (and others) who come here are higher than the incomes of their brother and sisters who stay put. The EHRC Report, struggling a bit with its traditional adversarial negativism, tells us that: 'although people from an Indian background are less likely than white people to have savings, when they do have savings, their median value is almost identical to the value of savings held by white people, at £3,000'.[10]

There follows the inevitable *however*, in this case as in: 'However, adults from other ethnic minority backgrounds tend to have lower value savings than white people'—no figures are given, though there is a reference. The 'however' continues: 'The median value of savings held by black people is the lowest of all the five groups covered by the FRS, at £2,000 (note sample sizes are small, i.e. black people N=108)'. 'FRS' is the Family Resources Survey. Interestingly enough, in Figure 12.2.1 on page 481, in an uncommented-on bar chart, we see that the only ethnic group where women of working-age are more likely to have a private pension than their men-folk is the black ethnic group. Whether we are considering pensions or savings, it is surely relevant to take into account the very high proportion of female-headed black households and the related tendency of many black men to be somewhat 'disassociated', shall I say, from domesticity: one half of black British children live in single parent mostly female-headed households.[11] The Report tells us that black Caribbean women are more likely to be in full time employment than *any other* group of women.[12] Surely, at this point, some comment about cultural incongruities would not be amiss? The EHRC has little wisdom to shed on these most interesting facts, indeed no more about this than about its finding that Pakistani and Bangladeshi women are three times as likely as white men and women *not* to have a bank account.[13] We are told, in yet another shuffle of responsibility, that: 'Some religious and ethnic groups may be excluded from credit by a lack of the availability of loans on terms that conform to their beliefs': where, on the 'Fairness Scale', does such a comment place Britain, credit providers or people with 'beliefs'?

Chapter 12 has several pages on 'wealth'. It also has a section on housing. I own the house in which I live: and when I die most of what I am 'worth' will be that property. In the section on 'wealth' there are figures for 'wealth inequality' between various ethnic and religious groups.[14] I assume that the figures include housing. Whether or not this is so, the later discussion of housing makes no mention at all of the type of tenure (the crucial variable) by ethnic and/or religious group. Many years ago, I wrote a short pamphlet entitled *Asian Housing in Britain*.[15] This showed that by 1978 Asian households (undifferentiated) were 70 per cent owner-occupiers, with whites then at 55 per cent and all households at 54 per cent. Inevitably, the Commission for Racial Equality, one of the EHRC's progenitors, assured us that such Asian households owned mainly old terrace houses, that they were in them only because of exclusion from council housing; or because they were denied mortgages; and that the old terrace houses they were forced to buy were not only lacking in basic amenities but that they were incapable of being modernised and that, in sum, such housing of and for Asian households was proof 'by any definition of severe housing need'.[16] Sadly, the EHRC continues with this nonsense, and in so doing undermines the very success of Asian households in buying and occupying property. *Social Trends Number 39*, 2009 edition, Table 10:8, shows that 73 per cent of Indian households living in England own their homes, either outright or with a mortgage, and the figure for Pakistani households 64 per cent; for white British, 73 per cent; for other whites 52 per cent; for Bangladeshis 37 per cent; all households 70 per cent. There is little point in going into detail: but if there are, say, 250,000 British-Indian households owning property valued at the UK average of about £200,000, then they own a total estate worth approximately £50 billion. The actual value will, of course, be a function of where the family lives: and property values can go down as well as up. It has taken the indigenous white population over a century to reach this level of wealth tied to owner-occupation.

This level of asset accumulation is all the more remarkable when we consider the Report's finding that labour force participation levels are low for (in particular) Pakistanis and Muslims. On page 401 we are told that 35 per cent of Pakistani men are in full-time employment (I resist an 'only') and that 10 per cent are in part-time work, while 21 per cent are self-employed: total 66 per cent, compared to 80 per cent for Indian, white British and other white men, whose rates of full-time employment are double those of Pakistani men. Analysed by religion[17] only 47 per cent of Muslim men and 24 per cent of Muslim women are employed, thus amongst other things having low rates of joint income. Muslims have the lowest recorded rates of employment in the UK. They have the highest rates of self-reported ill-health.[18] Yet 64 per cent of Pakistani households, who are nearly all Muslim, own their own homes. My own research, conducted in the mid-1980s, showed that some 'Asians' (undifferentiated) were also landlords in a big way, owning 54 per cent and 41 per cent of residential property in two parts of Newcastle upon Tyne. Only on page 651 does the Report (for the first time) mention 'growing home ownership' and 'growing material wealth'—phrases introduced though with the familiar 'however', this time referring to 'a persistent gap between the richest and poorest'.

Wealth, income, savings and pensions, wages, benefits, capital assets—all of these things are famously difficult to assess. The annual or monthly income of ethnic minorities is no doubt spent (as it is with most people) on annual or monthly necessities. Yet there is a 'surplus', unmentioned by the EHRC Report, the surplus which makes an appearance in the life of ethnic minorities as *Remittances*. Anyone wandering about areas of high minority settlement will notice the large number of banks and other organisations advertising a facility for sending money 'back home'.

The World Bank reckons that globally about $300 billion flow out as remittances from the developed and richer countries to countries like, but in no way exclusively, Pakistan, India and Bangladesh. This 'outstrips private capital and official aid in many countries: remittances account for 50 per cent of Pakistan's foreign exchange income, 10 per cent of Pakistan's labour force works overseas.[19] Most of it comes from migrants—and the money, obviously, flows from the richer countries to the poorer, with oil-rich Middle Eastern countries pulling in many thousands of workers from places like Pakistan and India. Remittances, at $250 millions according to Russell King, are over double the amount of overseas development assistance.[20] No doubt (as we are frequently told) migration was called into being by the need for labour. Equally, though, migrants responded because they needed the money, the money they could not get by staying at home: migration was and is mutually beneficial.

Migration is not random: many of the Pakistanis living in England came originally from Mirpur, and most Bangladeshi people living in England from Sylhet. These two regions are now amongst the wealthiest in their respective countries—thanks in large measure to remittances. Approximately £6 billion is sent every year out of the UK.[21] In the 'New Guidance' produced by the Department for International Development, Bangladesh is described as having almost half of household income being derived from remittances. There may well be, as the EHRC tables indicate,[22] 'unfairness' in the distribution of incomes and savings in Britain, with Pakistani and Bangladeshi households amongst the lowest in the tables. Not all of this can be explained by the different age and occupational structures of the population. Yet there still seems to be a substantial capacity to remit money 'home', due no doubt to a high propensity to save. The EHRC Report does not deal with this—unless I have missed it—but making some assumptions about the number of Pakistani households, and where the remittances actually go, then an average of approximately £600 per family may well be the amount sent back every year to India, Pakistan or Bangladesh.

This is indeed 'heroic' as Harriet Harman told a meeting in South London, a meeting held, if the *Telegraph* has it right, to advise immigrants on benefits how to send money home.[23] There has been some concern about predatory and corrupt money-men and money-transfer systems: and in 2010 the Department for International Development launched new guidance by the FSA entitled 'moneymadeclear', offering advice for people sending remittances. The then Exchequer Secretary to the Treasury Sarah McCarthy-Fry said: 'In Bangladesh almost half of monthly income can be made up of remittances'. International Development Minister Gareth Thomas said 'remittances are a vital source of income in many poor countries'. The main ones receiving remittances from the UK include India, Pakistan, Nigeria, Jamaica and Ghana.[24]

In December 2010 the *Daily Telegraph* reported on 'abroad fraud', that is people who, while in receipt of social security benefits, move abroad to live, whether to work or not. The Department for Work and Pensions estimate that in one year this cost £66 million. The four main 'homes' for the recipients are Spain, America, Bangladesh and Pakistan.[25]

In a variety of ways, then, Unfair Britain makes it possible for life to get a little fairer for the hard-working and other inhabitants of Pakistan, India and Bangladesh.

11

Rights of the State, 'Rights' in Society

Human rights, being universal by definition, are not the privileges of citizens, but the entitlement of all individuals... It is not a shared passport which motivates individuals to respect human rights and the corresponding responsibilities but a shared humanity.

Bikhu Parekh, *The Future of Multi-Ethnic Britain*[1]

Rights present themselves as absolute claims, 'trumps' as Ronald Dworkin call them. They cut a path through the complexities of moral deliberation—consideration of consequences, weighing of conflicting principles—and make a direct appeal to unconditional entitlements. When rights conflict, there is no language of resolution. Instead, all too often, there is violence, protest and direct action.

Jonathan Sacks, *The Politics of Hope*[2]

Right, in its full sense, is altogether an abstract thing which is independent of human laws and regulations; *claims* and *privileges* are altogether connected with the laws of society.

George Crabb, *English Synonyms*[3]

A recent Mayoral 'Citizenship' ceremony, held in the Civic Centre at Newcastle upon Tyne, saw several dozen assorted foreigners turned into citizens of the United Kingdom through the amiably-conferred ministrations of the Lord Mayor, a series of mumbled Oaths of Loyalty and a somewhat precarious rendition of one verse of 'God Save our Gracious Queen' (a Christian hymn as well as our national anthem). In a post-ceremony chat, I learnt that for some of them (mostly African) the assumption of British citizenship was a matter of almost redemptive joy: Free at last, Thank God (and the Lord Mayor) we are free at last! For others, it was matter of almost sullen personal convenience, rather like that of a friend of mine, an Iraqi Kurd, for whom the possession of British citizenship made it less dangerous and thus possible for him to return to Iraq to pursue a property dispute, having behind him (*qua* British citizen) the resources of the British Consulate to counterbalance the minatory presence of his quarrelsome relatives. In these various ways, and in a formal sense, and for sundry purposes, a collection of foreigners become citizens *just like me*, the equal beneficiaries of whatever rights I possess, all of them and all of us of equal legal status in this, the land of my birth. I experience this as a form of bad manners. With the backing of organisations like the EHRC, these new citizens acquire a legal status equal to mine! However (!) I know that in no way would (nor could) the Lord Mayor (a friend of mine) consider that he was able, through his office, to confer upon my new fellow-citizens the full inheritances, possessions and obligations of my birth, of (as Mr Phillips might put it) my parentage, my race, my nation, my gender, my age, my religion, my beliefs or my physical abilities and disabilities. The fact that I failed the 'Official Citizenship Test' (passed by my Slovakian daughter-in-law!) diminishes by not one thousandth of an inch my ineluctable existence in and obligation to the society and history of Great Britain. 'Rights' in this 'story' are beyond the casual conferment of the state or the possession of a mere passport. The rights, or, more properly, the privileges, which are sought *of society* are not easy to obtain. They are privileges which have to be earned, over generations: and in no other way.

Per contra, the array of rights claimed by both Phillips and Parekh can be authenticated only in and by a state, into which a passport is indeed, *pace* Parekh, the means of entry. The 'rights' so adamantly insisted on by the EHRC *can be demanded only of a state,* an organisation of which it is nowadays relatively easy, here and in much of Europe, to become a formal member.

Rights of the state: Lord Parekh, Mr Phillips

How fair to Great Britain is '*How Fair is Britain?*'? The moral or ethical power of this Report (as with the bulk of multicultural or equality literature) is derived from its version of 'Rights'—Human Rights, Minority Rights, Individual Rights. In the foreword to the Report, Mr Philips talks about 'the fundamental right of the individual' and of 'inalienable human rights':[4] his Commission, of course, has 'Rights' in its title. The contemplation of 'Rights' has long been a preoccupation of political philosophers, ethicists and theologians: but the magnificent originality of this Report is the way it reifies this abstract debate by interring it in the empirical plausibilities of table after table of statistics, bar charts, graphs and survey data. Going into this cornucopia at page 1 and exiting at page 750, the reader is inevitably persuaded of the 'unfairness' of 'discriminating', in Britain, against (or in favour of?) any (statistical) minority, no matter what that minority is and no matter what it may have done. As 'humans', intra-minority cultural differences are deniable and denied; as humans with 'rights' their entitlements are all the same and transcend all failings; and as humans with rights but no responsibilities (since EMFI Three is as absent from page 750 as it is from page 1), then the only possibility of being 'Fair' is to concede that we still have a long way to go before this country is, indeed, fair. Criticism applies only to the majority, their human rights being rendered inoperative precisely because they are a majority.

Mr Phillips provides the metaphysic for this remarkable doctrine: he tells us on 19 January 2009 that his:

> … mission is to ensure that, even in the worst of times, our destiny is not limited by our origins. That our life chances are not merely the sum of our parents' backgrounds and the racial or gender category into which we were born. That our success or failure does not become the hostage of age, religion, belief or disability.[5]

This is surely more theology than sociology or political theory: Mr Phillips conceives of humans as existing independently of their *birth*, their *race*, their *gender*, their *age*, their *religion*, their *belief* or their *physical competence*—his 'list', above: and on such human beings, so conceived, he is able to confer Rights no matter where they live or how or when they were created or what they have done or do. There is an imperial innocence in such a view, as it confers upon human beings a colonising legitimacy indifferent to all the boundaries created by birth, race, gender, etc: a scramble not merely for Africa but for everything. Such a conception of rights is, of course, of a long pedigree: and is totally compatible with the EHRC's and Lord Parekhs's promulgated 'terms of settlement' of ethnic minorities coming to the UK since the end of the Second World War. The progenitor of the EHRC, the Parekh Commission, proclaims that:

> Human rights, being universal by definition, are not the privileges of citizens, but the entitlement of all individuals... It is not a shared passport which motivates individuals to respect human rights and the corresponding responsibilities but a shared humanity.[6]

The introduction of the word 'passport' is significant. The most abstract conception of statutory rights, as in both of the above quotations, is obviously fully congruent with the political purposes of Mr Phillips and Lord Parekh, that is the irrefutable right of human beings, *qua* human beings, to full possession of the legal rights which exist (fortuitously or providentially, temporarily or permanently) here in the UK—or indeed anywhere else.

Deny this principle, then the matters about which the EHRC Report (and Parekh Report) are so fluent become arguments about mere convenience, of little moral force, suggestions rather than proclamations, a grouse not an outrage. When dressed in the apparel of rights, human rights, then there is no valid way of refuting or moderating the parade of 'inequalities' and 'injustices' contained in such Reports—until one makes the quiet but obvious point that rights are not, in actuality, experienced as absolutes, but always in small amounts: and that they depend for their lived-in power not on their mere enunciation but on specific secular arrangements, which vary all over the world: the passport counts, no matter what Lord Parekh thinks: so do human differences. Rights without passports have as much utility as a bath without water.

Yet, as we have seen in Chapter Ten, what is conferred by the British state is well worth having. We live in a state in which:

> there is no longer a normative trajectory of education, employment, heterosexual marriage, setting up a home and having children. Deviations from this pattern are expected and carry little or no stigma—it's all down to the individual.[7]

Perhaps, then, there is no need to be so sceptical about rights. After all, whatever they are, few of them are denied here in the UK. This is not an abstract quasi-philosophical debate, but an empirical one: never have we lived so lightly pressed or constrained by either circumstance or human coercive power. In the fair UK, an individual fate is more the result of individual choice than of outside force. Never have we lived at a time when so little penalty or blame or punishment attaches to deviancy, or difference—or even outright parasitism and disloyalty. Our present Prime Minister, David Cameron, is devising, as part of the responsibility of central government, a Well-Being Index, a happiness measure. His Big Society is clearly aimed at bringing amiability closer to home, on the streets where we live. Such minimal punitive purpose as is left to the central state is to be found in the ruse of forcing us to be free. The logic of the EHRC's insistence on 'fairness', on 'rights' is to legitimise this form of helpful coercion.

On pages 20-21 of the EHRC Report are listed 20 major pieces of legislation within which human rights are embedded. There are now over 35 Acts of Parliament, 52 Statutory Instruments, 13 Codes of Practice, 3 Codes of Guidance and 16 European

Commission Directives which bear on 'rights' and their associated issues of discrimination or unfairness. In 2010 I wrote a short book, *A New Inquisition,* in which I told the story of a Liverpool couple, Ben and Sharon Vogelenzang, whose livelihood was destroyed when the Crown Prosecution Service decided to accuse them (wrongly, said the judge eventually) of the crime of 'Religious Hatred'. Also in Liverpool, there is a citizen of the United Kingdom, Harry Taylor, who has been ordered by the courts not to carry with him, as he goes about his daily business, any literature which is hostile to religion. Mr Taylor is an atheist, rendered mute, but free, perforce.

Paradoxically, perhaps, the state springs doubly-armed from the pursuit of rights: and rights return the compliment. Implicit, and often explicit in nearly every table of the EHRC Report, is this type of demand, a demand made on and of the state. Thus, for example, we read in the last line of the Chapter 6 Summary of the Report about the 'failure *on the part of the state* to safeguard the lives of people from different groups equally' (emphasis added). The EHRC report is a thorough-going statist document: and in making these demands *of the state,* the EHRC has found an effective and expeditious way of explicating and enforcing Rousseau's *General Will* (appearing perhaps as Mr Cameron's *Big Society?*). No one elected the Equality and Human Rights Commissioners—indeed, they were all appointed well before the government which sanctioned them was removed from office. The Commission remains, creating and disseminating its version of the 'rights' of citizens (or of 'humans' or of 'individuals' or of 'minorities' or 'inalienable'—

whichever suits). Rarely are 'obligations' mentioned, or 'duties', other than my obligation or duty to recognise and genuflect to the promulgated rights of my new fellow-citizens. Rights are a licence to gatecrash the state. They remove gratitude. And the rights of the state are steadily being pushed into and colonising the proper realm of the antecedent society.

Over 150 years ago we were warned of this habit of democracy:

> Every day it [the state or 'power'] renders the exercise of the free agency of man less useful and less frequent; it circumscribes the will within a narrower range and gradually robs a man of all the uses of himself. The principle of equality has prepared men for these things; it has predisposed men to endure them and often to look upon them as benefits.[8]

De Tocqueville, genius though he was, was wrong to locate these things in the 'tyranny of the majority'. What we have here is the deliberate manufacture, by a set of self-interested creamy layers, of Rousseau's 'General Will', a blanket of shallow but pervasive self-serving 'public' morality. James Kalb describes this process wherein the state, for impeccably liberal reasons, moves into and colonises the once-free lands of society. He writes that:

> to implement such a programme of social transformation an extensive system of controls over social life has grown up, sometimes public and sometimes formally private, that appeals for its justification to expertise, equity, safety, security and the need to modify social attitudes and relationships in order to eliminate discrimination and intolerance.[9]

De Tocqueville, wrong perhaps in identifying the cause of what is happening, is, along with James Kalb, correct in describing what is going on. Rousseau got there first. Rousseau was in favour of such a process.

'Rights' in society

A world in which rights are derived from or demanded of the state will eventually become, as Kalb and de Tocqueville warned, intrusive, seductive, fractious and subtly oppressive. When demanded of the state, rights are easy to summon, to obtain and to impose upon others. They are comfortable things to demand, they are itchy and bad tempered things with which to try to live:

> [the proposed Racial and Religious Hatred Bill] would disproportionately curtail freedom of expression, worsen community relations as different religions and belief groups call for the prosecution of their opponents, create uncertainty as to what words or behaviour are lawful and lead to the selective application of the law in a manner likely to bring it into disrepute.[10]

Quite right: Messrs Cameron and Clegg both supported this condemnation of the 2006 attempt to legislate for 'religious hatred'.

We quoted above (p. 29) Thomas Paine, who distinguished between 'society' and 'government'. George Crabb makes the same distinction, associating 'claims and privileges', but not rights, with the laws *of society,* and not the state.

The rights, or more properly *the privileges* which are sought *of society* are neither easy to obtain nor easy to live with. There is no passport into society; no Lord Mayor could wand you into it. Mr Phillips and Lord

Parekh, refusing to be 'limited' by birth, parentage, race, nation, gender, age, religion, beliefs or physical abilities, will prove incompetent advisers to anyone seeking access to this real and concrete society, with its real and concrete privileges and responsibilities. Mr Phillips's list, though presented only to be denied, is, whether he knows it or not, that which defines *a society*. The 'limitations', however he disparages them, are the determinants (but not the sole determinants) of membership of a society. In denying them, he denies us (and somewhat limits his chance of joining). This is, of course, precisely what he wants: rights can be demanded of 'Britain', a piece of geography, a state, but not so easily or perfunctorily from the British, *a society, a history*. Indeed, it is not within the untrammelled power of the present generation so freely to confer upon anyone privileges and prerogatives constructed in and on, and often at the expense of, the lives of previous generations and in which the state itself is embedded. Into such a society I, like everyone else, come, at birth, as an immigrant. Into my development comes, through the stories of my family and people, me—and mine: through the development of my *birth, race, gender, age, religion, belief* and *physical competence* (the Phillips List!), I begin to become a member of this, this specific, society. My understanding of my inheritance is an understanding not of rights but of responsibilities and obligations, of obligations grounded in gratitude, gratitude to the men and women whose lives and names appear on street signs, grave stones, war memorials, school registers, public inscriptions, monumental buildings, pauper graves, single word epitaphs, great dramatic speeches, scoundrels, comedians, heroes and heroines, myths, legends, Boys Own Stories, archives of tragedy and of triumph, of errors and of attainments and, everywhere and more importantly, the great explicit anonymity of our collective achievement over many centuries. I have no great heroes or heroines in my family, though the semi-mythical stories of my Welsh ancestors abound in such things. My great grandfathers and great grandmothers, and my grandfathers and grandmothers were ordinary people who worked hard for their family, their communities and their country.

> Let not Ambition mock their useful toil,
> Their homely joys, and destiny obscure;
> Nor Grandeur hear with a disdainful smile
> The short and simple annals of the poor. [11]

Everywhere I am surrounded by these annals, an extraordinary inheritance of public wealth and societal competence and decency—roads, kerbs, taps, drains, museums, libraries, bin wagons, hedges, allotments, public parks, footpaths, clean water, art galleries, public meetings, chapels, sewers, traffic lights, a common language, a common religious vocabulary. My privileges derive from my ancestors who made these things, and such privileges are demeaned when called 'rights'. My privileges are but small and petty things in comparison to my obligations to the predecessors who made my society. This society, this socio-political culture (it is hard to find the appropriate word) is necessarily the slow unsteady outcome of many centuries of work, struggle, pain, failure, a precarious but real achievement. Some of my ancestors emigrated, most stayed, worked and died here. David Rollison tells us that:

> ... in 1500 fewer than three million people spoke English: today English speakers number at least a billion worldwide... The 'English explosion' was the outcome of a long social revolution with roots deep in the medieval past. A succession of crises from the Norman Conquest to the English Revolution were causal links and chains of collective memory in a unique, vernacular, populist movement. The keyword of this long revolution, 'commonwealth' [denotes] a panoramic synthesis of political, intellectual, social, cultural, religious, economic, literary and linguistic movements... in which state institutions and power elites were subordinate and answerable to a greater community that the early modern English called 'commonwealth' and we call 'society'.[12]

This story, on its own, makes our society possible. Further, when seen as such, our search for a legitimate presence in this country should more properly be seen as a search for *obligations* than for rights, building on what Burke referred to as 'a partnership not only between those who are living, but between those who are living, those who are dead, and those who are to be born'.[13] Our national society is a device for rationing privilege, not for distributing rights. Nothing is said in the EHRC Report about obligations, duties and loyalties, those human values which alone make society possible. Rights, in the world of the EHRC, come through the demanding of them. The EHRC simply does not understand, or if it does, prefers to render mute, the truth that rights demanded as of right by people who haven't earned them and who may not deserve them are diminished by the demanding: and that rights demanded of the state will soon enough become obligations and vexatious burdens imposed by the state. *Human* rights? It is easy enough to be human. It is much harder to be British.

To recognise the primacy of our national culture over our state would of course require that bodies such as the EHRC not only recognise the existence of that culture: they would have to accord it *Respect*—I use, with due and considerable diffidence, the semi-slang language of multiculturalism and of the EHRC. Nothing invokes the expostulatory stridencies of multiculturalism more than a suggestion that we, here, in this piece of the West, have created something of value, something (dare I say it?) better than those lands from which so many people have come since the end of the Second World War: why else do they come, and, having come, stay? Not only is it better: it is highly idiosyncratic, a particular, a singular, a *mono* where the EHRC and its associates would insist on seeing *multi*. This national culture is peculiar to these islands and the people (my people) who, in varying degrees, have occupied them for thousands of years. To even say this is of course to commit an offence. To say that this national culture is, currently, better than many of the others in the world, is to commit *another* offence, that of 'triumphalism', associated with predatory imperialism, our history, a history of what we did *to* the world. We are told that whatever *was* wrong in the world was due to our inability to stay where we came from: and whatever *is* wrong in the world is due to our continuing baleful influence. The EHRC and its predecessors seek to instruct us so as to internalise guilt: then, once we are redemptively re-configured, the settlement here of new cultures (*multi*) is not only a proper resolution of our long-owed debts to them, but also a salvific solvent of our grubby *mono* habits, a re-construction of a better past and a better future. We are invited to be ashamed of ourselves. Perhaps. Perhaps not.

At no point does the Report address the problem of its own making: the lack of attention to 'Equality Measurement Framework Indicator Three' (EMFI 3). Of all of the defects in this Report, this is surely a major one. To remind ourselves: EMFI 3 is as follows:

> Inequality of **autonomy** (i.e. inequality in the degree of empowerment people have to make decisions affecting their lives, how much choice and control they really have given their circumstances).[14]

Even given the demureness of the phrasing—'*really have*' provides an escape route big enough for a herd of elephants—EMFI 3 surely raises the question of *responsibility*. In the circumstances in which you find yourself, what do *you* do? What have *you* done? What, as Karl Marx might put it, have *you* done to make your own history under conditions not of your own choosing? The problem for the authors (and readers) of this Report is that the endless cascade of the language of rights in the state obscures the issue of responsibility to society: *If I have this opportunity, or this facility,* ***as of right****, then I do not have to earn it.* As privilege, I have to earn and re-earn it every day. This seems fair enough to me.

Epilogue

It pleases me to stand in silence here;
A serious house on serious earth it is,
In whose blent air all our compulsions meet,
Are recognised, and robed as destinies,
And that much never can be obsolete,
Since someone will forever be surprising
A hunger in himself to be more serious,
And gravitating with it to this ground,
Which, he once heard, was proper to grow wise in,
If only that so many dead lie round.

Philip Larkin, *Church Going*[1]

Larkin finds himself in a church. He takes off his bicycle clips in 'awkward reverence' because he thinks (rather than knows) that this is the proper thing to do in a church. He looks around and sees the evidence of a fading faith, kept alive by fusty buildings, wilted flowers and the paraphernalia of archaic rituals. Few people ('dubious women', 'Christmas addicts') now know the full meaning of all this: but like Larkin they do 'know' what they no longer believe, i.e. what they *disbelieve*. Then Larkin asks: 'And what remains when disbelief has gone?' He answers in the last stanzas, quoted above.

Some years ago, I published *The Christian Warrior in the Twentieth Century*,[2] which found in Europe's war memorials an answer, complementary to Larkin's, to the question about 'disbelief'. In the tens of thousands of war memorials to be encountered in public dedicated space all over Europe (indeed, all over the world), are the dead who define the 'serious earth' which we Europeans occupy. Through the experience of war, I wrote then, and through the war-related symbolisms of its Christian religion, i.e. war memorials, we visualise and live within 'Eurochristianity':

> Europe has an archaeology, a series of underlying strata of experience and belief which together make up the boundaries of a distinctive cultural inheritance and identity. Of the experiences, the most fundamentally formative is war. Of the beliefs, the most hauntingly evocative is the Christian religion. Together, they create a Eurochristian identity, a bellicognizant but not bellicose sense of the place of Europe in the world, of its fate and destiny, and of the nature of the moral trajectory of Europeans over their own continent as well as into the continents and lives of nearly all the other cultures of the world.

We are, I argued, neither bellicose nor pacifist: the millions of dead are seen as *giving* their lives—the word '*gave*', in most European languages, is the summation of how we remember the 'serious house on serious earth' of our terrible wars.

These wars, recalled and remembered in these ways, have re-configured the pattern of European enmities: these war memorials invite and insist on amity, of a weary kind perhaps: but not revenge: and an amity based on the shared experiences of war and horror. My father served in the Royal Air Force when it was engaged in the bombing of Germany and of its men, women and children. Inconceivable to me.

In the magazine *Standpoint*,[3] editor Daniel Johnson interviewed Necla Kelek, a Turkish-born German sociologist. They were discussing a book by Thilo Sarrazin called *Germany Abolishes Itself*. In this interview Ms Kelek described Germany as 'a treasure… our constitution, our democracy, the gift of freedom…

Germans value liberty particularly highly'. Is this, I said to myself, the same Germany that killed my mother's brother, that shot and imprisoned my father's brother, that was the recipient of bombs provided by the airmen of Bomber Command, of whom my father was one? The same Germany that in two wars killed the hundreds of young men with the same patronymic as me, names inscribed on war memorials all over Wales and elsewhere? The same Germany which had earlier in the twentieth century joined up with Austria-Hungary and the Muslim Ottoman Empire to close the Black Sea and to blockade Russia so as to prolong the Great War, thus leading to the deaths of hundreds of thousands of men and (arguably) leading also to the invention in the East of a new totalitarianism? The same Germany which in my lifetime gassed Jews—men, women and children? Surely, the sooner this Germany is abolished the better? Yet this Germany is indeed a 'treasure', even to my jaundiced mind. Over a full century, and through the grim and terrible oscillations of European patterns of enmity, we have come to 'know' both enemy and selves, in full and painful confessional, of the things we have done and left undone, offences committed through our own deliberate fault. Germany, for better or for worse, is part of my social identity: and 'Germany' and its European equivalents and opposites, nice and nasty, are close to who I am in a way in which, say, Amazonian Pirahas, Kikuyu elders, Hindu gurus, Arab kings and dhow captains are not. They, no doubt, are as real to themselves as I am to me and to my European nature and enculturation. It is in considering this culture (and the possible abolition of Germany) that we, like Amazonian Pirahas, Kikuyu Elders, Hindu Gurus and Arab dhow captains in their worlds, make some valuation of where we have come from, what we did, what we had done to us, where we are now and where we might wish to be.

Lest this be dismissed as mere triumphalism (or, worse, parochialism!) I will quote from the Epilogue to my book of 1995, *The Christian Warrior in the Twentieth Century.*

> If the post-modernists are correct, the strong tendency of Western civil culture is away from a subscription to the values and virtues of Grand Narrative—away, that is from an heroic, masculine and transcendent set of values—and towards one of value-indifferent hedonism. Such a culture may be able to live secure in its global hegemony, comfortably possessed of a disproportionate share of the world's wealth. It may, on the other hand, find its boundaries assailed by the dispossessed and the enraged of the world, pressing on the eastern and southern boundarics of Eurochristianity, either for admission as labourers or as would-be invaders. The zones of friction, to the south and east, are those where Eurochristianity confronts Islam.

How fair is Britain? How fair are our prospects when post-modern subsidised oracles like the EHRC preach and praise rights but not duties, when we are invited by such prophets down an endless series of false and petty claims, demands, loud clamorous and paltry mutterings about 'injustice', the pursuit of hedonism, all with an official face? It is to wave no arrogant flag nor to bad-mouth or slander other peoples to say that we, in our boring British European way, are, for the time being, both real enough and fair enough for most purposes: and fair enough for those people who want to come here and fair enough for those amongst them who, having come, most evidently want to stay and bring up their families here. They are welcome. We may of course, with or without them, be unable to maintain our relative stability. It adds little to the chances of maintaining this domestically amiable and globally useful position to give house-room and resources and serious attention to the EHRC and to the production of its paltry catalogue of complaint. The EHRC should be abolished.

Bibliography

Alibhai-Brown, Y., *The Settler's Cookbook: a memoir of love, migration and food*, Portobello Books, 2008, p. 423.

Bangladesh News, 10 February 2010, bdnews24.com

Birt, Y., *Being a Real Man in Islam: drugs, criminality and the problem of masculinity*, www.crescentlife.com. See also City Circle 25 March 2011, 'Young Muslim Offenders—Why Do They Keep Going Back to Jail?', at sid@thecitycircle.com. City Circle is a regular discussion group of (mostly) young Muslims.

Bruckner, P., *The Tyranny of Guilt, an Essay on Western Masochism*, Princeton University Press, 2010, p. 12.

Burke, E., in Conor Cruise O'Brien's *Edmund Burke*, London: Random House, 1997, p. 221.

Central Intelligence Agency, *World Fact Book* for November 2010, CIA website. The CIA provides up-to-date information on nearly all of the countries of the world.

Collins-Mayo, S., *The Faith of Generation Y*, Church House Publishing, 2010, p. 17/8.

Congdon, T., *Times Literary Supplement*, 24 March 2010 reviewing David Willetts's *The Pinch*.

Crabb, G., *English Synonyms*, Routledge and Kegan Paul, first published 1816, 1982 edition, pp. 604-05.

Davies, J.G., *Asian Housing in Britain,* The Social Affairs Unit, Research Report 6, undated.

Davies, J.G., *Bonfires on the Ice: the multicultural harrying of Britain,* The Social Affairs Unit, 2007.

Davies, J.G., *In Search of the Moderate Muslim,* The Social Affairs Unit, 2009.

Davies, J.G., *A New Inquisition: religious persecution in Britain today,* Civitas, 2010.

Davies, J.G., *The Christian Warrior in the Twentieth Century,* The Edwin Mellen Press, 1995, p. 1 and pp.142/3. See also 'War Memorials', in Clark, D. (ed.), the Sociological Review Monograph, *The Sociology of Death,* 1993.

Dennis, N., *Racist Murder and Pressure Group Politics: the Macpherson Report and the Police,* CIVITAS, 2000.

Eades, J. (ed.), *Migrants Workers and the Social Order,* ASA Monograph 26, Tavistock, 1987, chapter by Ballard, R., 'The Political Economy of Migration'.

Equality and Human Rights Commission, *HOW FAIR IS BRITAIN?, Equality, Human Rights and Good Relations in 2010, The First Triennial Repor*t, from www.equalityhumanrights.com

GLOBAL DATA

Below are listed a few of the many sources for 'global' data covering most of the world's countries.

Freedom House: Freedom in the World;
http://www.freedomhouse.org/template.cfm?page=363&year=2010

Institute of Peace and Economic Studies, The Global Peace Index, published by the Institute of Peace and Economic Studies;
http://www.visionofhumanity.org/gpi-data/
and
(http://ourtimes.wordpress.com/global-peace-index/#alpha

MSN Encarta, The Capital Punishment Index,
http://www.newworldencyclopedia.org/entry/Death_penalty

Transparency International provides data on corruption;
http://www.transparency.org/policy-research/surveys-indices/cpi/2010/results

The Press Freedom Index, published by Reporters without Borders;
en.rsf.org/spip.php?page

The World Economic Forum produces the Global Competitiveness Index;
www3.weforum.org/docs/WEF_GlobalCompetitivenessReport_2010-2011

The Legatum Prosperity Index 2010;
http://www.prosperity.com/countries.aspx

The Observer Human Rights Index; http://www.guardian.co.uk/rightsindex/

The UN's Human Development Index; http://hdr.undp.org/en/statistics/indices/hdi/

Gorer, G., *Exploring English Character*, The Cresset Press, London, 1955, pp. 213/15.

Government Equalities Office, 20 October 2010.

Government Office for the North East: Seminar on *Forced Marriage: Child Protection Implications for Education Practitioners*, Centre for Life, Newcastle upon Tyne, 16 March 2009.

Great Black Britons, website; www.100greatblackbritons.com/bios/stephen_lawrence.html

Gray, Thomas, 'Elegy Written in a Country Churchyard', in Palgrave, F.T., *The Golden Treasury*, Thomas Nelson and Sons Ltd, 1943.

Green, D., *We're (Nearly) All Victims Now! How political correctness is undermining our liberal culture*, CIVITAS, 2006.

Home Office Research Study 294 Assessing the Impact of the Stephen Lawrence Inquiry, HO Research, Development and Statistics Directorate October 2005.

House of Commons Committee of Public Accounts, *Equality and Human Rights Commission, HC* 124, March 4 2010.

Inspector Gadget, *Perverting the Course of Justice, the hilarious and shocking inside story of British policing,* Monday Books, 2008.

International Organisation for Migration, the migration agency, email hq.iom.int

Kalb, J., *The Tyranny of Liberalism,* ISI Books, 2008, p. 6.

King, R., *The Atlas of Human Migration; global patterns of people on the move,* Earthscan, 2010, pp. 98-99.

Kynaston, D., *Austerity Britain 1945-51,* Bloomsbury, London, 2007.

Larkin, P., *Church Going,* in Black, E.L. (ed.), *Nine Modern Poets,* Macmillan, 1966.

Macpherson of Cluny, Sir William, *The Stephen Lawrence Inquiry,* Cm. 4262-1, and 4262-2, 1999.

Marquez, M., quoting Mrs Lawrence, at a conference on Multiculturalism in Europe and America, Charles University, Budapest, Summer 2002, downloaded 1 December 2010.

Mills, C.W., *The Sociological Imagination,* OUP, New York, 1959, p. 151.

Milton, L. and Aspinall, P., *Black Africans in the UK: Integration or Segregation, unpublished,* available at l.milton@kent.ac.uk

Morgan, K.O., *Rebirth of a Nation: Wales 1880-1980,* OUP, University of Wales Press, 1982, pp. 108-12.

National Audit Office, *Report on the accounts of the EHRC,* 20 July 2009; http://www.nao.org.uk/publications/0809/ehrc_accounts.aspx

National Archive, the UK The National Archive: Department for International Development, 'New Guidance on Remittances', 9 February 2010.

Norton, P., *The British Polity,* 2nd edn, New York and London: Longman, 1991, p. 347.

Paine, T., *Common Sense,* 1776. In the Millennium Library Thomas Paine, Everyman's Library, Introduction by Michael Foot, 1994, p. 251.

Parekh, Bikhu (now Lord), *The Future of Multi-Ethnic Britain,* Runnymede Trust Report of the Commission on the Future of Multi-Ethnic Britain, Profile books, 2000.

Phillips, T., Speech at Leeds Social Sciences Institute, 17 June 2008, downloaded 3 November 2010; www.equalityhumanrights.com/key-projects/speeches/trevor-phillips-speech-at-leeds-social-science

Phillips, T., 'Institutions must catch up with public on race issues', 19 January 2009, downloaded 16 November 2010; http://www.equalityhumanrights.com/key-projects/race-in-britain/event-ten-years-on-from-the-macpherson-inquiry/stephen-lawrence-speech-institutions-must-catch-up-with-public-on-race-issues/

Phillips, T., New Commission poll shows British institutions need to 'keep up with Obama generation', 20 January 2009; http://www.equalityhumanrights.com/news/pre-june-2009-new-commission-poll-shows-british-institution

Porter, B., *The Absent-minded Imperialists: Empire, Society and Culture in Britain,* OUP, 2004.

Rollison, D., *A Commonwealth of the People, Popular Politics and England's Long Social Revolution, 1066-1649,* pre Title Page, CUP, 2010.

Rose, J., *The Intellectual Life of the British Working Class,* 2nd edn, Yale University Press, 2010.

Rousseau, J-J., *Du Contrat Sociale,* livre 1, chapter vii, Du Souverain, Garnier Freres, Paris, 1962, p. 246,

Sacks, J., *The Politics of Hope,* Random House, 1997, page 29.

Saunders, P., *Difference, Inequality and Unfairness: the Fallacies, Errors and Confusions in the EHRC Report,* October 2010, Civitas Online.

Social Trends, No 39, 2009 edn, ONS website.

Straw, J., Ministry of Justice, 24 February 2009, downloaded 1 December 2010; www.justice.gov.uk/new/speech240209a.htm

Tocqueville, A. de,. *Democracy in America,* the Henry Reeve Text, edited by Phillips Bradley, Alfred Knopf, NY., 1976, vol. 2, pp. 318ff.

UK The National Archive: Department for International Development, 'New Guidance on Remittances', 9 February 2010.

UN
World Bank: Migration and Remittances; http://web.worldbank.org

Notes

Foreword

1 Parekh, Bikhu (now Lord), *The Future of Multi-Ethnic Britain,* Runnymede Trust Report of the Commission on the Future of Multi-Ethnic Britain, Profile books, 2000.

2 For a discussion of the role of cultural theory in the recent historiography of the British Empire, see Porter, B., *The Absent-Minded Imperialists,* OUP 2004, *passim* but especially Ch. 1, 'Empire and Society'.

3 Parekh's formulation may be contrasted with the classic statement by the American jurist Oliver Wendell Holmes (in Arnheim, M., *Principles of the Common Law,* London, 2004, p. 111): 'The first requirement of a sound body of law is that it should correspond with the actual feelings and demands of the community, whether right or wrong.'

4 Parekh, *The Future of Multi-Ethnic Britain,* point 3.30, p. 38.

5 For Parekh's discussion of British history see *The Future of Multi-Ethnic Britain,* Ch. 2, 'Rethinking the National Story', pp. 14*ff.*

6 Geertz, C., *The Interpretation of Cultures,* Basic Books, 1973, pp. 259-60.

7 Parekh, *The Future of Multi-Ethnic Britain,* p xiv.

8 Sen, A., 'Reason Before Identity', the Romanes Lecture for 1998, OUP, 1999, p. 25.

9 Sen, 'Reason Before Identity', p. 20.

10 Collier, P., *Wars, Guns and Votes,* London: Harper, 2009, p. 185.

1 The EHRC Report

1 Phillips, J., Leeds Social Sciences Institute, 17 June 2008, downloaded 3 November 2010; www.equalityhumanrights.com/key-projects/speeches/trevor-phillips-speech-at-leeds-social-science

2 *How Fair is Britain? Equality, Human Rights and Good Relations in 2010: The First Triennial Review*, EHRC, 2010, p. 12; www.equalityhumanrights.com

3 Saunders, P., *Difference, Inequality and Unfairness: the Fallacies, Errors and Confusions in the EHRC Report*, October 2010; http://www.civitas.org.uk/pdf/Saunders_EHRC_ReportBriefingOct2010.pdf

4 *How Fair is Britain?*, pp. 482, 648.

5 *How Fair is Britain?*, p. 403.

6 *How Fair is Britain?*, p. 162.

7 Norton, P., *The British Polity*, 2nd edn, New York and London: Longman, 1991, p. 347.

8 Radio interview, reported in *The Sunday Times*, 9 January 2011.

9 The Muslim Council of Britain, Press Release, 'MCB Welcomes Conviction of Sex Offenders but Urges Caution on Racialising Crimes', 8 January 2011.

10 *The Times*, 17 January 2011.

11 *How Fair is Britain?*, p. 222.

2: Mr Phillips's Baggage—Mislaid?

1 Mills, C. W., *The Sociological Imagination*, New York: OUP, 1959, p. 151.

2 *How Fair is Britain? Equality, Human Rights and Good Relations in 2010: The First Triennial Review*, EHRC, 2010, pp. 70-71.

3 Central Intelligence Agency, *World Fact Book* for November 2010, CIA website. The CIA provides up-to-date information on nearly all of the countries of the world.

4 Milton, L., and Aspinall, P., *Black Africans in the UK: Integration or Segregation,* unpublished, available at l.milton@kent.ac.uk.

5 Saunders, P., *Difference, Inequality and Unfairness: the Fallacies, Errors and Confusions in the EHRC Report*, October 2010; http://www.civitas.org.uk/pdf/Saunders_EHRC_ReportBriefingOct2010.pdf

6 See *How Fair is Britain?*, pp. 81, 94.

3: Of Human Rights and Human Equality

1 Parekh, Bikhu (now Lord), *The Future of Multi-Ethnic Britain,* Runnymede Trust Report of the Commission on the Future of Multi-Ethnic Britain, Profile books, 2000, p. 106.

2 Trevor Phillips, Leeds Social Sciences Institute, 17 June 2008.

3 Paine, T., *Common Sense*, 1776. In the Millennium Library Thomas Paine, Everyman's Library, Introduction by Michael Foot, 1994, p. 251.

4 *Daily Telegraph*, 20 November 2010.

5 Rousseau, J-J., *Du Contrat Sociale*, livre 1, chapter vii, Paris: Du Souverain, Garnier Freres, 1962, p. 246. [My translation, with the aid of Dr David Place and Professor Gerard Docherty.]

6 Parekh, *The Future of Multi-Ethnic Britain*, p. xx.

7 *Sun*, 16 November 2010.

8 *Daily Telegraph,* 16 November 2010.

4: The Origins of the EHRC

1 Government Equalities Office, 20 October 2010.

2 *Pink News,* 3 July 2010.

3 Macpherson of Cluny, Sir William, *The Stephen Lawrence Inquiry,* Stationery Office, Cm. 4262, February 1999.

4 *Guardian,* 23 November 2010.

5 See Porter, B., *The Absent-minded Imperialists: empire, society and culture in Britain,* OUP, 2004.

6 Parekh, Bikhu (now Lord), *The Future of Multi-Ethnic Britain,* Runnymede Trust Report of the Commission on the Future of Multi-Ethnic Britain, Profile books, 2000, p. 21.

7 Davies, J.G., *Bonfires on the Ice: the multicultural harrying of Britain,* The Social Affairs Unit, 2007.

8 Foreign and Commonwealth Office, the Home Office, and MCBDirect, *Muslims in Britain,* 2004.

9 *Muslims in Britain.*

10 Davies, J.G., *A New Inquisition: religious persecution in Britain today,* Civitas, 2010.

11 Davies, J.G., *In Search of the Moderate Muslim,* The Social Affairs Unit, 2009.

5: Lord Parekh and his Report

1 Parekh, Bikhu (now Lord), *The Future of Multi-Ethnic Britain,* Runnymede Trust Report of the Commission on the Future of Multi-Ethnic Britain, Profile books, 2000, p. viii.

2 *Guardian,* 23 November 2010.

3 Parekh, *The Future of Multi-Ethnic Britain,* p. 26.

4 Parekh, *The Future of Multi-Ethnic Britain,* p. 27.

5 Parekh, *The Future of Multi-Ethnic Britain,* p. 35.

6 Parekh, *The Future of Multi-Ethnic Britain,* p. 35.

7 Parekh, *The Future of Multi-Ethnic Britain,* p. xiv.

8 Parekh, *The Future of Multi-Ethnic Britain,* p. xiv.

9 Parekh, *The Future of Multi-Ethnic Britain,* p. 2.

10 Parekh, *The Future of Multi-Ethnic Britain,* p. 25.

11 Parekh, *The Future of Multi-Ethnic Britain,* p. 57.

12 Parekh, *The Future of Multi-Ethnic Britain,* p. 223.

13 Parekh, *The Future of Multi-Ethnic Britain,* pp. 296-314.

14 Bruckner., P., *The Tyranny of Guilt, an Essay on Western Masochism,* Princeton University Press, 2010, p. 12.

6: The Macpherson Report

1 Marquez, M., quoting Mrs Lawrence, at a conference on Multiculturalism in Europe and America, Charles University, Budapest, Summer 2002, downloaded 1 December 2010.

2 *Great Black Britons,* website; www.100greatblackbritons.com/bios/stephen_lawrence.html

3 Straw, J., Ministry of Justice, 24 February 2009; downloaded 1 December 2010; www.justice.gov.uk/new/speech240209a.htm

4 Home Office Research Study 294, 'Assessing the Impact of the Stephen Lawrence Inquiry', HO Research, Development and Statistics Directorate, October 2005.

5 Macpherson, W., *The Stephen Lawrence Inquiry,* Cm. 4262-I, 1999, Chapter 1:5.

6 See Davies, J.G., *A New Inquisition: religious persecution in Britain today*, Civitas, 2010, pp. 35-43.

7 Dennis, N., *Racist Murder and Pressure Group Politics: the Macpherson Report and the Police*, CIVITAS, 2000; and see also Green, D., *We're (Nearly) All Victims Now! How political correctness is undermining our liberal culture*, CIVITAS, 2006.

8 Macpherson, *The Stephen Lawrence Inquiry*, Chapter 2:15.

9 Macpherson, *The Stephen Lawrence Inquiry*, Chapter 6:15.

10 Macpherson, *The Stephen Lawrence Inquiry*, Chapter 6:15.

11 Macpherson, *The Stephen Lawrence Inquiry*, Chapter 6:34.

12 Macpherson, quoted in Parekh, Lord, *The Future of Multi-Ethnic Britain*, Profile books, 2000, p. 69.

13 Macpherson, *The Stephen Lawrence Inquiry*, Chapter 6:3.

14 Parekh, *The Future of Multi-Ethnic Britain*, p. 69.

15 Macpherson, *The Stephen Lawrence Inquiry*, Chapter 6:31.

16 Parekh, *The Future of Multi-Ethnic Britain*, p. 72.

17 Parekh, *The Future of Multi-Ethnic Britain*, p. 24.

18 Parekh, *The Future of Multi-Ethnic Britain*, p. 126.

7: Parekh + Macpherson = EHRC

1 Phillips, T., 'Institutions must catch up with public on race issues', 19 January 2009, downloaded 16 November 2010; http://www.equalityhumanrights.com/key-projects/race-in-britain/event-ten-years-on-from-the-macpherson-inquiry/stephen-lawrence-speech-institutions-must-catch-up-with-public-on-race-issues/

2 Phillips, 19 January 2009.

3 Decca Aikenhead, The G2 Interview, downloaded November 2010.

4 *Guardian,* 23 November 2010.

5 Alibhai-Brown, Y., *The Settler's Cookbook: a memoir of love, migration and food,* Portobello Books, 2008, p. 423.

6 *How Fair is Britain? Equality, Human Rights and Good Relations in 2010: The First Triennial Review,* EHRC, 2010, p. 576.

7 *How Fair is Britain?,* p. 576.

8 *How Fair is Britain?,* p. 588.

9 Phillips, 20 January 2009.

8: The EHRC—A Creamy Layer?

1 See Chapter 7 of Davies, J.G., *Bonfires on the Ice: the multicultural harrying of Britain,* The Social Affairs Unit, 2007.

2 *How Fair is Britain? Equality, Human Rights and Good Relations in 2010: The First Triennial Review,* EHRC, 2010, p. 588.

3 EHRC FO1419, by e-mail to me, 25 November 2010.

4 House of Commons, HC 124, 4 March 2010.

5 National Audit Office, *Report on the accounts of the EHRC,* 20 July 2009; http://www.nao.org.uk/publications/0809/ehrc_accounts.aspx

6 House of Commons, HC 124, 4 March 2010.

9: A Thin Blue Line

1 Gorer, G., *Exploring English Character,* London: The Cresset Press, 1955, pp. 213-15.

2 Gorer, *Exploring English Character,* pp. 213-15.

3 Gorer, *Exploring English Character,* pp. 213-15.

4 *Sunday Times,* 16 January 2011.

5 *How Fair is Britain? Equality, Human Rights and Good Relations in 2010: The First Triennial Review,* EHRC, 2010, p. 107.

6 *How Fair is Britain?*, Chapter 7, p. 148.

7 *How Fair is Britain?*, p. 220.

8 *How Fair is Britain?*, p. 205.

9 *How Fair is Britain?*, p. 205.

10 Government Office for the North East: Seminar on *Forced Marriage: Child Protection Implications for Education Practitioners,* Centre for Life, Newcastle upon Tyne, 16 March 2009.

11 *The Times,* 6 January and 9 January 2011.

12 Davies, J.G., *In Search of the Moderate Muslim,* The Social Affairs Unit, 2009.

13 City Circle, 'Young Muslim Offenders—Why Do They Keep Going Back to Jail?', 25 March 2011, at sid@thecitycircle.com. City Circle is a regular discussion group of (mostly) young Muslims.

14 Birt, Y, *Being a Real Man in Islam: drugs, criminality and the problem of masculinity,* 2001; www.crescentlife.com

15 *How Fair is Britain?*, p. 124.

16 See page 98 of my *In Search of the Moderate Muslim.*

17 Gorer, *Exploring English Character,* pp. 213-36.

18 Inspector Gadget, *Perverting the Course of Justice, the hilarious and shocking inside story of British policing,* Monday Books, 2008.

19 Norman D., *et al., Racist Murder and Pressure Group Politics: the Macpherson Report and the Police,* Civitas, 2000, p. xx.

20 *How Fair is Britain?*, pp. 174-75.

21 Emphasis added. Author's notes.

22 Author's notes, 24 July 2005.

23 Davies, *In Search of the Moderate Muslim*, pp. 91-109.

24 Birt, *Being a Real Man in Islam.*

25 Quoted in Davies, *In Search of the Moderate Muslim*, p. 101.

10: The Unfair World in Which We Live

1 International Organisation for Migration, the migration agency, email hq.iom.int; and King, R., *The Atlas of Human Migration; global patterns of people on the move*, Earthscan, 2010, pp. 98-99.

2 GLOBAL DATA. Below are listed a few of the many sources for 'global' data covering most of the world's countries.

Freedom House: Freedom in the World; http://www.freedomhouse.org/template.cfm?page=363&year=2010

Institute of Peace and Economic Studies, The Global Peace Index, published by the Institute of Peace and Economic Studies,
http://www.visionofhumanity.org/gpi-data/
and
http://ourtimes.wordpress.com/global-peace-index/#alpha

MSN Encarta, The Capital Punishment Index, http://www.newworldencyclopedia.org/entry/Death_penalty

Transparency International provides data on corruption, http://www.transparency.org

The Press Freedom Index, published by Reporters without Borders, www.en.rsf.org/spip.php?page

The World Economic Forum produces the Global Competitiveness Index; http://www.weforum.org/

The Legatum Prosperity Index 2010; http://www.prosperity.com/countries.aspx

The Observer Human Rights Index; http://www.guardian.co.uk/rightsindex/

The UN's Human Development Index; http://hdr.undp.org/en/statistics/indices/hdi/

3 http://ourtimes.wordpress.com/global-peace-index/#alpha

4 http://www.transparency.org/policy-research/surveys-indices/cpi/2010/results

5 www.en.rsf.org/spip.php?page

6 http://www.weforum.org

7 Congdon, T., *Times Literary Supplement*, 24 March 2010, reviewing David Willetts, *The Pinch*, Atlantic Books, 2010.

8 Morgan, K.O., *Rebirth of a Nation: Wales 1880-1980*, OUP, University of Wales Press, 1982, pp. 108-12.

9 Sunday Worship, BBC Radio, 21 November 2010.

10 *How Fair is Britain? Equality, Human Rights and Good Relations in 2010: The First Triennial Review*, EHRC, 2010, p. 468, Box 12.1.1.

11 *Social Trends Number 39*, 2009 edition, p. 16, ONS website.

12 *How Fair is Britain?*, p. 648.

13 *How Fair is Britain?*, p. 510.

14 *How Fair is Britain?*, pp. 471-72, Tables 12.1.5 and 12.1.6.

15 Davies, J.G., *Asian Housing in Britain*, the Social Affairs Unit, Research Report 6, undated.

16 See Davies, *Asian Housing in Britain,* p. 3.

17 *How Fair is Britain?*, p. 405.

18 *How Fair is Britain?*, p. 265.

19 World Bank: Migration and Remittances; http://web.worldbank.org

20 See chapter by Ballard, R., 'The Political Economy of Migration', in Eades, J. (ed.), *Migrants Workers and the Social Order,* ASA Monograph 26, Tavistock, 1987; and King, R., *The Atlas of Human Migration ; global patterns of people on the move,* Earthscan, 2010, pp. 98-99.

21 UK The National Archive: Department for International Development, 'New Guidance on Remittances', 9 February 2010.

22 *How Fair is Britain?*, pp. 468, 480.

23 *Daily Telegraph,* 13 December 2010.

24 *Bangladesh News,* 10 February 2010; bdnews24.com

25 27 December 2010.

11: The Rights of the State, 'Rights' in Society

1 Parekh, Bikhu (now Lord), *The Future of Multi-Ethnic Britain,* Runnymede Trust Report of the Commission on the Future of Multi Ethnic Britain, Profile books, 2000, p. 90.

2 Sacks, J., *The Politics of Hope,* Random House, 1997, p. 29.

3 Crabb, G., *English Synonyms,* Routledge and Kegan Paul, first published 1816, 1982 edition.

4 *How Fair is Britain? Equality, Human Rights and Good Relations in 2010: The First Triennial Review,* EHRC, 2010, p. 7.

5 Phillips, T., 'Institutions must catch up with public on race issues', 19 January 2009;

http://www.equalityhumanrights.com/key-projects/race-in-britain/event-ten-years-on-from-the-macpherson-inquiry/stephen-lawrence-speech-institutions-must-catch-up-with-public-on-race-issues/

6 Parekh, *The Future of Multi-Ethnic Britain*, p. 90.

7 Collins-Mayo, S., *The Faith of Generation Y*, Church House Publishing, 2010, p. 17/8.

8 Tocqueville, A. de, *Democracy in America*, the Henry Reeve Text, edited by Phillips, Bradley, NY: Alfred Knopf, 1976, vol. 2, pp. 318ff.

9 Kalb, J., *The Tyranny of Liberalism*, ISI Books, 2008, p. 6.

10 Opposition Motion to 'Not Read' the Religious Hatred Bill, supported by Messrs Cameron and Clegg, House of Commons , 21 June 2005.

11 Gray, Thomas, 'Elegy Written in a Country Churchyard', in Palgrave, F.T., *The Golden Treasury*, Thomas Nelson and Sons Ltd, 1943.

12 Rollison, D., *A Commonwealth of the People, Popular Politics and England's Long Social Revolution, 1066-1649,* pre Title Page, CUP, 2010.

13 Burke, E., in Conor Cruise O'Brien', *Edmund Burke*, London: Random House, 1997, p. 221.

14 *How Fair is Britain?*, p. 58.

Epilogue

1 Larkin, P., *Church Going*, in Black, E.L. (ed.), *Nine Modern Poets*, Macmillan, 1966.

2 Davies, J.G., *The Christian Warrior in the Twentieth Century*, The Edwin Mellen Press, 1995, p. 1 and pp.142-43. See also

'War Memorials', in Clark, D. (ed.), the Sociological Review Monograph, *The Sociology of Death,* 1993.

3 *Standpoint,* January/February 2011.